Twenty-First Century Socialism

T0056360

Jeremy Gilbert

———————

Twenty-First Century Socialism

polity

Copyright © Jeremy Gilbert 2020

The right of Jeremy Gilbert to be identified as Author of this Work has been asserted in accordance with the UK Copyright, Designs and Patents Act 1988.

First published in 2020 by Polity Press

Reprinted 2020 (five times), 2021 (twice), 2022 (twice)

Polity Press
65 Bridge Street
Cambridge CB2 1UR, UK

Polity Press
101 Station Landing
Suite 300
Medford, MA 02155, USA

ISBN-13: 978-1-5095-3655-9
ISBN-13: 978-1-5095-3656-6 (pb)

A catalogue record for this book is available from the British Library.

Library of Congress Cataloging-in-Publication Data
Names: Gilbert, Jeremy, 1971- author.
Title: Twenty-first century Socialism / Jeremy Gilbert.
Description: Medford : Polity, 2020. | Series: Radical futures | Summary:
  "In this urgent manifesto for a 21st century left, Jeremy Gilbert shows
  that we need a revitalised socialist politics that learns from the past
  to adapt to contemporary challenges"-- Provided by publisher.
Identifiers: LCCN 2019032308 (print) | LCCN 2019032309 (ebook) | ISBN
  9781509536559 (hardback) | ISBN 9781509536566 (paperback) | ISBN
  9781509536573 (epub)
Subjects: LCSH: Socialism--History--21st century. |
  Capitalism--History--21st century. | Populism--History--21st century.
Classification: LCC HX45 .G45 2020 (print) | LCC HX45 (ebook) | DDC
  335--dc23
LC record available at https://lccn.loc.gov/2019032308
LC ebook record available at https://lccn.loc.gov/2019032309

Typeset in 11 on 15 Sabon by Servis Filmsetting Ltd, Stockport, Cheshire
Printed and bound in the UK by TJ Books Limited

The publisher has used its best endeavours to ensure that the URLs for external websites referred to in this book are correct and active at the time of going to press. However, the publisher has no responsibility for the websites and can make no guarantee that a site will remain live or that the content is or will remain appropriate.

Every effort has been made to trace all copyright holders, but if any have been overlooked the publisher will be pleased to include any necessary credits in any subsequent reprint or edition.

For further information on Polity, visit our website: politybooks.com

Contents

Acknowledgements

This book wasn't one that I ever expected to write, although I'm glad I have, and it's only thanks to the persistence and patience of my colleagues at Polity – George Owers and Julia Davies – that it's come about at all. Keir Milburn and Alex Williams both read and commented on a first draft and were insightful and supportive as ever.

The phrase 'twenty-first-century socialism' obviously isn't one that I coined: it was being used in various publications from the late 1990s onwards, and probably much earlier. I used this phrase polemically once or twice before, but the first time I used it as the title for anything, it was at the behest of Craig Gent, who asked me to write a short piece on the topic for Novara Media that in some ways ended up becoming the intellectual kernel of this book. In broader terms, the present volume draws

Acknowledgements

on arguments that I've made in earlier, more academic work, such as my books *Anticapitalism and Culture* and, most importantly, *Common Ground*. Perhaps more immediately, it draws on commentary that I've written for publications such as *Soundings*, the *Guardian*, *Red Pepper* and *New Statesman* over many years – but above all for Open Democracy. Perhaps most directly it draws on the pamphlet 'Reclaim Modernity', which I wrote with Mark Fisher and which was published by the think tank and lobby group Compass in 2014. I'm grateful to all these outlets and to my editors, readers and collaborators there.

More than any of those sources, however, some of the book's key sections on the nature of capitalism and socialism and on the defining features of recent and contemporary history draw on my many years of teaching undergraduates at the University of East London. Teaching students on degree programmes in cultural studies, sociology, music, media studies, politics, history and English – trying to equip with them with a comprehensive and comprehensible account of how the world works and how it got that way – has often been a challenge, but always a rewarding one. It's a matter of great regret that most of those degree programmes no longer exist, but the many students who passed through them

Acknowledgements

are all owed a debt of gratitude for helping me to shape and hone much of the account and analysis offered here. So are my colleagues at the Centre for Cultural Studies Research at UEL, which thankfully persists in its commitment to public discussion, freed education and political analysis as well as to exploring the boundaries of cultural studies and cultural theory.

Above all, of course, like most writers, I owe a permanent debt of gratitude to my immediate friends and family for their ongoing support and inspiration. Jo Littler and our children – Robin and Isla – make every day special and make the future matter more than ever. It would really be impossible to list all the friends and colleagues who contribute to and stimulate my political thinking every day, but over the past few years friends connected to and taking part in the *Culture, Power, Politics* seminar series, as well as organisations and projects such as Compass, Momentum, The World Transformed, the New Economy Organisers Network and #ACFM have all been crucial sources of insight and interlocution. Many thanks to all of them.

Introduction

This book proposes that a twenty-first-century socialism is the only reasonable solution to the various crises and problems that the world faces today[1] – from social inequality to climate breakdown. In Part I the book sets out to explain what the basic source of those crises and problems is and why 'socialism' might be the solution to them. In Part II the book explores in greater detail the specific features and conditions that characterize the world we live in today, from the technological revolution to the capture of our cities by the super-rich. In Part III the book expounds what the specific characteristics of a twenty-first-century socialism would be.

Part I

Capitalism and Socialism

1

The Cause of the Trouble

'Socialism' is a word that was coined almost two hundred years ago.[1] In practice, it can mean many different things. But, in principle, it means something simple. It is the belief that the quality of human life can be improved if people are enabled and encouraged to cooperate for the common good, rather than being forced to compete among themselves for access to resources, power and status.

So why should anyone believe that this nineteenth-century philosophy could have the answer to twenty-first-century problems?

Because our major problems today have exactly the same cause as the major problems faced by people in the early 1800s: industrial pollution, urban squalor, growing inequality, social insecurity, a widespread sense that society was falling apart and that nobody knew what to do about it, while a few were getting very rich as a result.[2] Sounds familiar?

The Cause of the Trouble . . .

The most obvious cause of such problems is, always, technological change. The Industrial Revolution swelled the cities of Britain, poured smoke into the atmosphere and spelled the end of an older, agricultural way of life. In recent decades, the revolution in information technologies has made it possible for jobs to be relocated from one side of the planet to another at the click of a mouse, producing insecurity and inequality all around the world. Millions have been forced to migrate or reinvent themselves in the search for steady wages. Global trade – dependent on road, sea and air transport – has accelerated to the point where climate change threatens the very viability of life on Earth.[3]

But social changes like these are never simply the direct effect of new technologies. It was never inevitable that the invention of steam power, canals and railways would lead to grinding poverty in the cities of northern England. In the 1960s, many commentators assumed that the development of computing and robotics would make us all richer and happier: we would work shorter hours, communicate instantly, and be free to fill our days as we please, because machines would be doing most of the work.[4] Things could have turned out that way; but they didn't.

In each case, the way things have actually turned out has been the outcome of technological change taking place under very specific circumstances. Some people have made themselves rich and powerful mostly by using those technologies in order to make things and sell them.

But the best technology in the world cannot enable an individual entrepreneur, or a chief executive, to make and sell things without help from other people. Those other people have to be paid. And, if they are paid too much, it will not be possible for the entrepreneur or corporation to accumulate vast profits. So, for the most part, corporations and their chief executives used new technologies to try to keep down their wage bills, at their own workers' expense, whenever the opportunity presented itself.

Capitalism

For all this to happen, the social circumstances had to be right. There had to be a small group of people rich enough to use the new technologies in these ways. There had to be large numbers of people around who had no choice but to work for the wages that they were offered. There had to be a whole legal system in place, and a culture, that treated the accumulation of vast profits by private individuals or corporations as legitimate, legal, and morally acceptable. These conditions actually wouldn't have obtained in most human societies that we know to have existed since *Homo sapiens* first appeared as a species. But they did in many European countries by the end of the eighteenth century. And they soon would almost everywhere else.

There is a name for this specific set of social circumstances: 'capitalism'. This term refers to a situation in which private individuals or corporations are allowed to use any means available to them – short of openly violent coercion – to accumulate vast profits from the sale of commodities, even if, in the process, they are paying workers very low wages, wrecking the local environment, or forcing people to change their way of life against their will.

This was already happening in the early nineteenth century and is still going on today. It is in the pursuit of unlimited profits that corporations undertake fracking, chop down rainforests, and belch carbon dioxide into the atmosphere. When companies relocate manufacturing plants from one country to another – disrupting communities, spreading insecurity throughout the working population of a whole region – they very rarely do it because they absolutely have to in order to make any profits at all. They do it because, however much profit they are making at that moment, they will make even more if they move.

Why Is It Called 'Capitalism'?

'Capital', in the economic sense of the term, refers to wealth that exists in a form that allows it to be invested, or lent (and often this means the same thing), in the expectation of returning a profit: a profit that will take the form of more capital.[5] 'Capitalism' is a word that only started to be used towards the end of the nineteenth century, but the term 'capitalist' had already been around for decades, designating someone who profits from his or her ability to invest capital. And, at its simplest, 'capitalism' can mean only this: it can just be a word for what capitalists do, which is to invest capital with the aim of increasing their total stock of capital. As we will see shortly, 'capitalism' can also refer to a whole way of ordering society, and to a set of values and beliefs about how society should be ordered. But at its most basic it can simply refer to a type of activity: investing capital with the aim of accumulating profit in the form of more capital.

This is what economists call 'capital accumulation'. This isn't the same thing as merely making profits. If you generate a lot of profit, but you use it all to finance a luxurious lifestyle – or even just to keep yourself and your employees comfortable – then you are not necessarily doing capitalism. Capitalism is what you are doing once the accumulation of further capital becomes the principal objective of your activities. So 'capitalism' can just mean the pursuit of capital accumulation through investment.

But nothing is that simple. For one thing, even before Karl Marx (the greatest analyst of capitalism in the nineteenth century)[6] began writing, economists were clear that the profitability of such investment was generally dependent on capitalists employing workers, while paying them as little as possible for their work.[7] This doesn't mean that every business owner who employs a couple of dozen people is an enemy of the people. In fact it doesn't mean that such a person is necessarily a capitalist: if he or she is not engaged in a relentless pursuit of unlimited profit, then it might be that he or she is not really practising capitalism at all. On the other hand, it does mean that, even today, every profitable 'investment' that is derived from the pursuit of capital accumulation is always dependent on the exploitation of someone's labour somewhere. If your pension fund owns shares in Apple or Facebook – two organisations that are absolutely committed to capital accumulation – then the profits that accrue from those investments don't simply materialise out of thin air. They are dependent on the labour of actual human beings: assembling phones in China, coding in Bangalore, moderating ads from Menlo Park.[8]

A World of Commodities

So 'capitalism' is the practice of accumulating capital through the exploitation of wage labour to produce commodities for sale.

A commodity is anything that can be bought and sold for profit, and there have been commodities throughout recorded history. But in Europe a number of step changes occurred between the fifteenth and the nineteenth centuries. Colonialists 'discovered' new commodities such as tea, sugar and coffee; they also 'discovered' new populations around the world to whom they could sell other commodities (textiles in India, firearms in Africa, opium in China, etc.). The Industrial Revolution made possible the production of commodities on a completely unprecedented scale; it also disrupted rural economies based on subsistence farming and local crafts, leaving city dwellers having to buy all kinds of things (food, clothes, furniture) that they would once have made for themselves or acquired from a skilled neighbour.[9]

The result is that today we live in a society in which almost every object we ever touch is a commodity. This is a strange situation. Even in Britain, the first industrialised country, less than three hundred years ago most of the physical objects in most people's lives – their food, their clothes, their tools, everything – would have been made by themselves or by someone that they knew. Now we live in a world in which our entire material culture is a product of capitalism.

This has dramatic effects on how we relate to the world and to the other people in it. We are surrounded by all this stuff – everything from pens to cars to houseplants to icecreams – and all of it is made by people. Those people actually have to cooperate with one another on a vast scale in order

12

to make it and get it to us: their activities have to be coordinated in factories, in global distribution networks, in retail outlets and in packing warehouses. But all that cooperation tends to be invisible to us. All we see is the stuff. We tend to behave as if the stuff has come out of nowhere and has a magical life of its own. Marx called this 'commodity fetishism'.[10]

Capitalists accumulate capital only by selling commodities. This means that they are constantly motivated not just to sell the commodities they already have, but to invent new ones and to find new people to sell them to. In the early stages of colonialism and industrialisation, this was a straightforward and often brutal process. Europeans went to various other parts of the world and used their superior weaponry to gain access to the land of the people who were already living there, generally killing or enslaving those people in the process. They then forced those people, or slaves imported from Africa, to grow crops that people in Europe would buy. Back in Europe, wealthy people – many of whom were getting rich from this new form of international trade – increasingly used their wealth and influence to force peasants off the lands that their ancestors had farmed, so that they (the rich people, with a few hired labourers) could farm intensively, producing food to be sold for profit to a population that could no longer grow it for itself. Those peasants had no choice but to move to the expanding towns and cities, taking whatever work they could find, selling their labour in factories and using their wages to purchase a meagre selection of those commodities that they needed to keep themselves alive. An enlarging middle class consumed more and more luxury commodities – finer teas, more expensive clothes, ornate furniture. Until the late nineteenth century, most workers lived barely above subsistence level.

By the early twentieth century this all started to get more complicated. The working poor of the towns and cities had become organised and educated, formed unions and political parties, and had to be granted significant increases in wages and better standards of living. Most of their basic needs were met, so capitalists couldn't continue to expand their profits only by selling them necessities. European countries had made colonies everywhere they could and were starting to be pushed back, as the populations of those colonies became better educated and better organised. Even in the United States, westward expansion had reached its limit.[11] Capital accumulation could continue to expand only if people could be persuaded to buy more and more commodities that they hadn't previously needed.

The modern advertising industry came into being to persuade them to do just that,[12] and today we live in a world in which a large part of the culture that we are exposed to takes the form of someone's trying to sell us something. At the same time, capitalists looked for new ways to turn into commodities things that hadn't been commodities before. Over the course of the twentieth century and into our own, we have seen not just an incredible expansion of the number of things we can buy. We have seen many aspects of social life also turned into things we can buy. Caring for your elderly relatives, finding you a romantic partner, guiding you to inner peace: these and many other activities are now services that you can purchase as commodities from multimillion dollar industries. And all the while the production of material commodities has been increasing at an exponential rate by depleting the Earth's resources, by pumping carbon into the atmosphere. Everything from basic mineral resources to our ability to form relationships with other humans is now subject to the capitalist logic of *commodification*.

During the middle decades of the twentieth century, many countries saw attempts to remove essential social activities from the realm of commodity exchange. As governments took on responsibility for providing services such as education and healthcare, they were effectively 'decommodified'. But, since the 1970s, many of these public services have been privatised – that is, handed over to private corporations who are allowed to sell them for a profit, which brings them clearly into the domain of capital accumulation. Up until the twentieth century, for example, education was generally a commercial service; but it was not one provided by capitalists. Most educational institutions were private schools that generated income for their owners, managers and staff; but they were usually not instruments of full-scale capital accumulation. During the mid-twentieth century education was decommodified, as it became a universally available public service. What we have seen since the 1970s is a global wave of such services being commodified or *recommodified* in ways that allow for vast profits to be generated from them by international corporations.[13]

This process is typical especially of the 'neoliberal' politics that has informed most government programmes since the 1970s.[14] It also illustrates how the drive towards commodification and profit can have far-reaching social, cultural and political effects. For example, taken to its logical conclusion, the privatisation and commodification of education services completely transforms the nature of the relationship between teachers and students, changing it from a collaborative bond into a simple trade between a buyer and a seller. This is not a change that students, teachers, parents or community members generally have any cause to welcome – which is why the privatisation and semi-privatisation of education services is rarely popular, even though it has been happening around the world for decades.[15] Such privatisations have been possible only under specific political conditions, wherein corporations that stand to make millions from them have been able to exert extraordinary influence on government decisions.[16]

The Capitalist 'System'

This is why the term 'capitalism' is often used to mean something more than just the practice of accumulating capital through the exploitation of waged labour and the sale of commodities. 'Capitalism' in this sense can refer to an entire system for the production and distribution of material goods (what Marx calls a capitalist *mode of production*), or to an entire social order built around that economic system (what some theorists have called a capitalist *social formation*).[17] In any such social order, it will be the rich – the capitalists – who have the most power. They will use that power to pressure governments to enact policies that are beneficial to them, and will use their wealth to spread propaganda favourable to them and their interests. In countries such as the United States and the United Kingdom, wealthy capitalists spend hundreds of millions on lobbying governments and on acquiring control over media institutions (newspapers, websites, advertising agencies, radio and TV stations), and this gives them enormous influence over political outcomes.[18] At the same time, their ordinary activities as capitalists have more influence over the lives of millions of people than does anything that governments do; for these millions are the people they employ, the people who depend on those people, the people who work for companies that supply or are supplied by them, many of the people in the affected local communities, and so on. What I am describing here is a *plutocracy*: a society ruled by the rich.[19]

When we talk about 'capitalism' as an entire social order, these are the main characteristics that we should bear in mind: capitalism is characterised by the unlimited pursuit of capital accumulation, by the tendency to commodify resources and social relations, and by the tendency to generate a plutocracy. It's quite common to refer to a society in which these tendencies predominate as a 'capitalist society'. This is a useful shorthand. But it's worth sounding a note of caution here. The idea that we live in a 'capitalist society' can often lead to the assumption that 'capitalism' is a totally integrated and self-enclosed system, which subsumes every element of contemporary social life. Some theorists have certainly seen it this way. But this can be misleading. We live in societies in which capitalism has some effect on every aspect of social life and presents an obstacle to the realisation of many social goals. But there are all kinds of things going on all the time that are not capitalism, from teaching in public schools to the commercial activity of medium-sized businesses or to ordinary interaction between friends. Capitalists are absolutely committed to finding ways of using all these activities for the purpose of accumulating capital: they sell services to schools, lend money to businesses, mine every online conversation for data. But those activities can carry on perfectly well without capitalists or capital accumulation.[20]

This is why, when we make statements such as 'we live in a capitalist society', we should be careful. This can give the impression that the only way in which we could emancipate ourselves from capitalism at all would be to overturn completely the social system we inhabit. There might be times and situations when this is true. But there might also be times when resisting the encroachment of capitalism doesn't require such total transformation. Sometimes it can simply mean creating, defending or building up institutions that are not organised along capitalist lines – public libraries, non-commercial broadcasters, cooperatively owned social media platforms, the National Health Service, and so on – and pushing back against the inevitable capitalist attempt to take them over.

Capitalism or Capitalists?

There's a bit of an ambiguity in the way I've been describing 'capitalism', especially now that I've started to talk about 'resisting it'. Are we talking about actual capitalists here – specific wealthy individuals, the particular companies that they own – or are we just talking about a general way of doing things that can, overall, be described as 'capitalism'?

The answer is: sort of both. 'Capitalism' is best understood as a set of practices and a set of social relationships that emerge from those practices. In the twenty-first century, those practices can carry on even if hardly anybody engaged in them particularly thinks that capitalism is a good way of organising things. In principle you can find yourself to be the director of a major corporation, apparently engaged in the practice of pure capitalism, without having any personal belief that capitalism is actually a good thing to do.

This has led some theorists and commentators to conclude that it is simply naive to talk about 'capitalism' as anything but an abstract system – a kind of impersonal machine that just keeps going without anybody being in charge of it. This is partly true. But the danger of taking this too far is that such a view ignores some very basic facts about the world we live in. Capitalism has winners and losers. Jeff Bezos did not become a billionaire by accident. Nor did he become a billionaire simply because he played the capitalist game successfully, according to rules that he didn't invent. He became a billionaire by changing the game in such a way that the practice of capitalism could extend into more and more areas of social life. For example, Amazon has incorporated thousands of small businesses – businesses that had once been engaged only in sustainable commerce – into an all-inclusive system aimed at accumulating capital for one group of people in particular: Jeff Bezos, his senior executives, and Amazon's shareholders.[21] Capitalism is, at one level, an abstract system with nobody in overall control of it. But it is a system that would not exist without the continued efforts of capitalists to make themselves wealthy at everyone else's expense.

Liberalism and Neoliberalism: The Capitalist Story

None of this would be able to carry on unless capitalists had a half-plausible story to tell themselves and other people as to why what they do is fine and admirable. The most obvious version of this story brings us back to the issue of technology. 'Of course we're making the world a better place!' say the CEOs of giant tech corporations; 'just look at all the cool stuff we're giving you'. But was capitalism the only way we could have got all this cool stuff?

No. Even the most cursory investigation into the history of computing technology, networking, microchips and touchscreens will show you that in fact almost all the core research that made your smartphone possible was done either by publicly funded researchers (usually at universities) or by networks of amateurs and enthusiasts.[22] The story of almost every major technical innovation is that capitalists get involved only at the stage where the technology is already very close to being ready for the market: at this point they pay the inventors for the right to turn their ideas into commodities that they can hire workers (usually poorly paid Asian workers) to manufacture for them.

Not only do we not need capitalism in order to get technological innovations that everyone can use. There is good reason to assume that, if technologies such as the World Wide Web or the smartphone had been developed by non-capitalist organisations, they would probably not have developed their most harmful features. The interfaces of the smartphone and its apps are deliberately designed to make the smartphone as compulsively addictive as possible.[23] There's nothing inherent in the core technologies that makes this gadget so addictive. Those addictive features are put there on purpose, because the people who sell you the phones (together with the apps and the access to the platforms you will use them with) are not just out to make an honest profit from the sale. They are out to make as much money from you and to extract as much saleable data from you as they possibly can.

So even capitalists who do seem to bring us something worth having are not nearly as indispensable to the process as they would have us believe. But most capitalists aren't selling us cool technologies. Most of them aren't even manufacturers; they derive profits from speculation on shares, currencies, derivatives and debt instruments, or from retailing, distributing and marketing things that other companies have made, or from renting out property and land. What story can they possibly tell themselves, us, and governments around the world to convince enough people that their overweening wealth and power are anything but an intolerable affront to reason and human dignity?

The story they tell today is pretty much the same one that they've been telling for about four hundred years, since long before the Industrial Revolution, when European merchants first started to take over the rest of the world. It goes something like this: 'Human beings come into the world alone. They may collaborate with others to achieve certain goals or to protect their property, but their basic relationship with other humans is, at root, a competitive one. It is up to every individual to strive as best they can to enrich themselves, by working hard and deploying their unique talents. In a modern commercial society, governments will encourage them

24

to do just this, in the knowledge that by pursuing riches, entrepreneurs will bring improvements to the lives of their many customers (improvements like sugar, tobacco and social media). For such a society to function smoothly, and for entrepreneurs to remain motivated to play their crucial role, the state must make the protection of private property its number one priority. Property and those who hold it must not only be protected from marauding bandits or foreign invaders; it must be protected from any claims that the wider community might try to make on it. Taxation, public spending, the regulation of corporations and markets: these may all be necessary to a degree, but they must be strictly limited if society is not to descend into tyranny. Any society that puts strict limits on the ability of individuals or corporations to enrich themselves would be a tyranny, and tyranny is the worst thing in the world. Because it is wrong to put restrictions on the economic activity of entrepreneurs, decisions over things like the prices of goods or the value of labour (i.e. wages) must be left up to the market; while individuals and corporations must be allowed to use any means available to them (advertising, media propaganda, etc.) in order to pursue their commercial interests and protect them from interference by either competitors or the wider public.'[24]

This way of looking at the world is so closely associated with capitalists and their interests that, sometimes, when people say 'capitalism', what they mean is simply this set of beliefs. It would be accurate to say that this worldview is the one that most capitalists espouse and try to propagate. It is also a worldview that, if everyone believes it, will serve capitalists and their interests very well indeed, because it makes capitalism appear to be the most natural, obvious and beneficial way of organising social relations, and even the natural world. This is what it means to say that this worldview expresses a capitalist *ideology*. However, it's not really accurate to call that particular view of the world 'capitalism'. Such a view is more accurately described as 'liberalism'.[25]

In the United States, in the mid-twentieth century, the term 'liberalism' came to be used as a catch-all for any kind of politics committed to social reform, from women's rights to extensive welfare programmes. This is a misleading use, however. Properly speaking, 'liberalism' is the name for a political tradition and a set of attitudes that, in theory, put the rights of individuals ahead of the claims of community, tradition or state. Liberalism values individual freedom, privacy, autonomy and property. In theory. In practice, that generally

26

means putting the rights of privileged individuals ahead of those of everybody else[26] – because it's much easier to exercise your personal freedom in the world if you are rich, white and male than if you are none of these things. To be fair, generally liberalism at least allows people who aren't rich, white and male to protest their situations, and even to make arguments as to why they should be allowed to exercise the same freedoms as those who are, which is certainly preferable to fascism.

Liberalism itself can take various forms, from the brutality of Britain in the 1830s, when traditional protections for the poor were abolished because middle-class taxpayers didn't want to pay for them, to the egalitarian social reforms of the mid-twentieth century. Since the 1970s, governments around the world have enacted programmes informed by 'neoliberal' ideas and policies. 'Neoliberalism' is a widely used and sometimes misused term today. It was coined in the 1930s, but neoliberal ideas were not put into practice by governments until the 1970s. In a nutshell, neoliberalism is the most explicitly and aggressively pro-capitalist version of liberalism ever formulated. Where liberals tend to assume that being a self-interested, competitive entrepreneur is the natural state for human beings, neoliberals know that it isn't. But that's still how they want people to behave. So they want to use both the state and corporate power to force us to behave like that, whether we like it or not.[27]

Neoliberals want students to compete with one another in school and schools to compete with one another, like businesses in a marketplace; and they will force them to behave that way by whatever means necessary. They want every possible social relationship to be commodified and monetised. They want culture to be produced for profit and for no other reason at all: they don't care about 'the arts', they just want to see profitable 'creative industries'. They want every aspect of your personality to be judged good or bad not according to any objective or socially approved scale of value, but according to how far you can or cannot render it profitable. Do you have a winning smile? Become an Instagram influencer. Are you angry about something? Make ranting videos and sell ads on your YouTube channel. Do you want healthcare? Then you should pay for it the same way you would pay for a house or a hamburger.[28]

Neoliberalism strives towards these ends through its basic political imperatives: privatise public services, deregulate labour markets (so workers have fewer rights and protections), attack labour unions, cut taxes on the rich, contract public spending and welfare entitlements, and force those services that remain in the public sector to behave, as much as possible, like competitive, profit-seeking businesses. All this is designed to produce a world in which everyone is perpetually insecure and people are obliged to think of themselves as competitive entrepreneurs in every aspect of their lives: work, school, dating, spirituality, friendships, even family.[29]

Why do neoliberals want this? Because if everyone – or even just enough people – accept that this is the way the world works, then they will accept a world ruled by bankers.[30] Only in a world where every aspect of life is treated as a speculative asset will we accept that those who actually make things, have ideas, help people or teach people should all be subservient to those whose only skill consists in turning speculative assets into capital.

We live in such a world today. And this is the cause of most of the problems with literally everything.

2

Why Socialism?

The basic claim of socialism is that the world should not be run by a tiny clique of capitalists who act solely in their own interests, but by all the people on the planet, as they work and think together for the common good. Socialism has a very different understanding of humans and their relationships from that found in the capitalist story. It also happens to be an understanding that is far more grounded in material, historical and scientific reality.

The fact is that humans have only ever survived and prospered in cooperation, both with one another and with the wider environment. Even under capitalism, the vast work of material production upon which modern life depends rests on a set of entirely cooperative relationships between workers – in factories, in transportation and communication, in retail and administration.

Why Socialism?

Capitalists want workers to compete for jobs, because that way capitalists can offer workers lower wages. Capitalists also compete with each other, to maximise those profits. But none of this is necessary, or usually even helpful to the actual work in hand. Capitalists get their profits and their power from their ability to organise the cooperative activity of millions and from the chance this gives them to act as middlemen between, say, the workers in the retail outlets and the workers in the factories.

But, with help from sympathetic governments and with innovative forms of organisation, we could just cut out those middlemen.[1] We could then take away those vast profits that capitalists siphon off for themselves; and we could use them so as to make everyone's lives better and the planet healthier and safer.

This is the basic socialist idea. Human life and creativity are inherently social and collaborative.[2] Cooperation is generally more productive, dynamic and efficient than competition. Capitalism distorts this reality. It brings people together to cooperate in vast productive enterprises, but insists that the results of this cooperation must be, always and only, commodities to be sold for a profit in the marketplace rather than things or services that all people get to use because they need them or because they want them. Capitalism forces people to compete for access to resources that they themselves have helped to create; under neoliberalism, it even takes resources that were collectively produced and publicly managed – such as public education systems or water-processing facilities – and hands them over to capitalists to administer at will, commodifying them, profiting from them, making them harder for everyone else to access.

Socialism doesn't propose to remake human nature. Conservative and liberal propaganda often claims that this is the trouble with socialism: it wants to take the messy, selfish, intractable reality of human beings and to try moulding it into some vision of the perfect society. There are forms of totalitarian socialism that attempt to do that. But, as we've already seen, neoliberalism, too, wants to force people to conform to its ideal model of the competitive entrepreneur. Most forms of socialism don't want to do this at all. In fact, what they want is to find ways of allowing more people to benefit from the cooperative processes in which they are *already engaged*, in almost every aspect of their lives, and to have a say in the management of those processes.

So the most basic aim of socialism is to establish productive social relations on a cooperative basis. Exactly how this is to be done is another question, of course; and there are many possible answers. One persistently popular method, imagined since the mid-nineteenth century, is to call for the state to take over direct control of key industries, infrastructure and services, from railways to healthcare to the steel industry. Such a view has often led to the assumption that socialism simply means control of industry by the state. But this is true only to the extent that the state itself is seen as a genuine collective expression of the will and intentions of the wider community. In the Soviet Union and the countries that followed its model, the state claimed to direct all social activities towards the common goal of enriching the whole society. Socialist critics, however, always argued that its political structures were so hierarchical and dictatorial that they did not facilitate the truly cooperative relations that genuine socialism would require.

Another interpretation of the socialist idea is that people should belong to economic organisations that are not simply incorporated into the state but are organised along cooperative, democratic and relatively egalitarian lines. The ideal of the workers' cooperative – a productive organisation owned and managed by its workers – has had many adherents, at least since the nineteenth century.[3] There are many different types of workers' coops. Some could be large corporations that are managed in an entirely conventional way but happen to have no shareholders. These corporations use all their profits to pay the employees, who are in effect the company's shareholders. In practice, however, even coops that are large commercial organisations, such as the John Lewis Partnership in the United Kingdom, are administered far more democratically than most corporations. Other coops are radically egalitarian institutions in which all management decisions are taken collectively and democratically. A related idea, also originating in the nineteenth century, is that of syndicalism, according to which the basic unit of political organisation in the socialist movement should be the radical trade union; and these unions would eventually take over the management of the industries in which they were based. Arguably the most successful socialist economy in modern history was that of post-war Yugoslavia, where citizens worked for independent enterprises that were owned and managed by workers, in the context of a market economy overseen by a government that prohibited large-scale private profits and capital accumulation.[4] All these are variations on the idea that the cooperative relations sought by socialism can be organised in a different way from that of having centralised state institutions direct all economic activity.

The NHS

Most modern societies contain at least some important institutions that have a more or less socialist character. A famous example is Britain's National Health Service (NHS), which provides full healthcare for all citizens. This healthcare is directly funded by central government, is free at the point of use, and is delivered in publicly funded and managed facilities.[5] The NHS puts relations within the healthcare sector onto a cooperative basis, not in the sense of being managed in a radically democratic or egalitarian fashion, but at least in the sense that the object of all the activity it oversees is the improvement of the patients' health – an objective towards which all its employees collaborate, without anybody seeking profit from the exercise. Of course, many private providers of medicines, goods and services do profit from it and, since the onset of the neoliberal era in the 1980s, have been allowed to do so to a far greater extent than previously.

There are a few important things worth noting about the NHS. Apart from the fire brigade, it is the most popular and trusted institution in the country. Most British people simply regard the fire service as utterly heroic (without knowing that the Fire Brigades Union is one of the most consistently radical unions in the country); but everybody knows that the NHS is a politically distinctive institution.[6] At the same time, it is a more or less unique institution within the British welfare state. As in many other countries, in the United Kingdom most of the welfare state was established over the course of the twentieth century on a social-insurance safety net model. The idea is that pensions, unemployment benefits and housing are all provided to a minimum standard for those who can show themselves to be in the greatest need and who have made specific relevant contributions through the tax system. The NHS is not like that. It is a universal service, which provides all aspects of healthcare to everyone on the basis of need and is paid for entirely from direct taxation.

Most British people have a sense that the NHS is different from other public institutions, in the United Kingdom and elsewhere. What few of them realise is that there is a specific political history to this difference. Many know that the NHS was introduced in the 1940s by the reforming Labour government led by Clement Attlee, that it was created partly in response to the recommendations of

Why Socialism?

the Liberal Party grandee, William Beveridge, and even that its chief architect was the Welsh minister for health and housing, Aneurin Bevan.[7] What is less well understood today is that 'Nye' Bevan, a radical socialist, had to fight for this socialist model of the NHS against opposition even from within his own party, the most conservative sections of which would have preferred a system more in line with the principles that informed the rest of the welfare settlement. Bevan was a pragmatist, but also a radical socialist with a political base in the most militant section of the British working class: the miners of the South Wales coalfield. He modelled the NHS on a mutually owned medical aid society based in the Welsh mining town of Tredegar, of which he himself had been a member.

It is very unlikely that Bevan would have been able to win the fight to 'Tredegarise' the United Kingdom, as he famously put it,[8] had it not been for the fact that, at the time, the South Wales miners were at the peak of their political power, as the post-war labour shortage, the dependency of the British industrial economy on coal, and the political radicalism of the miners themselves – many of them influenced by communism, the experience of industrial militancy in the 1920s, the struggle against fascism since the 1930s, and radical popular education – all fortuitously converged. I doubt that, without the political leverage that his base in the South Wales coalfields gave him, Bevan would have been able to push through his programme of implementing the fully socialist NHS that Britons are still so fond of today.[9]

The most popular political institution in Britain is popular because it is the country's most genuinely socialist institution; and it is that thanks to the militancy and radicalism of what was probably the most radical and politically committed section of the working class in British labour history.[10] Not many British people know that. It would be a very different country if they did.

Decommodification: Building the Commons

The NHS is not the most radically organised institution in the world. In the 1970s, the Labour government responded to demands for users of the service (which is almost everyone in the United Kingdom) to have more of a say in its administration by creating locally elected 'community health councils' (CHCs) to interact with NHS management. The CHCs were abolished by Tony Blair's government in 2003, replaced by powerless, corporate-style 'consultation' forums attended by randomly selected service users.[11] But, while the NHS is not particularly democratic, it does exemplify a key feature of a socialist political institution in that it removed healthcare in the United Kingdom from the domain of profitable commodity exchange – not completely (for that to happen, the entire pharmaceutical industry would have to be publicly owned), but insofar as it is experienced by most citizens.

A key objective of socialism has always been to push back against the commodifying tendency of capitalism. From a socialist perspective, not all forms of commodification or market exchange are necessarily bad. The commercial drive to invent new things for profit, to trade and to exchange can have many positive effects in the world. But capitalism tends to impose commodification where it isn't needed or wanted. Most readers will be familiar with the idea that essential social services should be decommodified; and, when asked, most citizens of modern democracies seem to agree. But we can also ask ourselves whether anybody apart from very wealthy individuals actually benefits from, say, basic foodstuffs being supplied as commodities in a marketplace rather than being provided collectively, by the whole community, to the whole community.

If you want to buy artisanal sourdough from your local independent bakery – that's great. But if you just need a basic, industrially produced sandwich loaf to feed your kids, why shouldn't it be provided for free, or at cost price, by a publicly owned industrial bakery? Who benefits otherwise? And how is this less essential than education or healthcare?

Decommodification is one of the key objectives that all forms of socialism share, although there will always be differences over what needs to be decommodified and how. It's easy enough to see how this line of thinking applies to healthcare and education, and even to bread. But it's also relevant for thinking about other topics. Around 1999–2000, the global music industry was thrown into crisis by the emergence of MP3 file-sharing technologies. This raised a problem both for the artists themselves and for the corporations profiting from their work: file-sharing was, effectively, decommodifying music – making it into something that couldn't be bought and sold for profit because everyone could get it for free.[12]

Since that time, in place of the old system whereby record companies sold physical commodities (records, cassettes, CDs), a new one has been installed whereby customers pay for access to vast databases of files that they either download or stream. Of course, it's no surprise who benefits most from this. The income derived by artists – the people actually making the music – is considerably lower now than it used to be, because corporations like Apple and Spotify pay very, very small royalties for individual streams and downloads, while those corporations are now worth billions. What has happened is that music has been effectively *recommodified* in a new form, in a way that only increases the wealth and power of those capitalists able to profit from this new form, and without benefitting the creative producers of the music very much at all.

This is the kind of problem that socialist decommodification would seek to solve. Just think about it for a moment. The systems that have been created by giant platform companies to distribute music to users are fantastic. They make a universe of music available to listeners and give artists the chance to reach millions at the click of a mouse. But there is absolutely nothing inherent in the technology used by those platforms to suggest that their distribution mechanisms have to operate in a capitalist fashion. iTunes and Apple Music could be owned cooperatively by every user of the service in return for paying a small subscription fee (as they already do for Spotify or Apple Music). Artists could still be paid per stream or per download; but they could be paid far more than they currently are if most of those payments weren't being directed to Apple or Spotify shareholders. A more radical variant of the same system might see artists' rewards kept within a reasonable range, to allow for more income to be directed to supporting newer and less well-known musicians. Presumably there would have to be some kind of minimum threshold of popularity for an artist to receive support, but this and similar policy decisions could be made democratically by all users of the service. An even more radical version might see the entire system operating like this, while being funded and supported by governments, in order to guarantee access to all citizens.

All these measures would contribute in some measure to a transformation of the general field of music culture from a capitalist marketplace into a *commons*. A commons is a set of resources that are collectively owned and, to some extent, democratically administered by all of the people who depend upon them. The NHS, for example, transforms healthcare from a system governed at every level by the logic of commodity exchange into a system that can, at least partly, be considered a commons.[13]

Why Socialism?

Democratise the World

This little thought experiment about a socialist music system brings me to the third key feature of any socialist programme. Such a project will not only seek to promote cooperative social relations and institutions and to decommodify certain areas of social life, building commons; it will do so with the explicit aim of reducing inequalities of wealth and power, wherever they may be found. It will attempt to disaggregate concentrations of wealth and power, working to disperse power and distribute resources more equitably in many different social situations. In particular, it will try to do so in such a way as to give power over the systems of production and distribution to those most directly involved in them or most directly affected by them. In the hypothetical example I just considered, the enormous concentration of wealth and power in the hands of a couple of corporations and their owners (and shareholders) would be dispersed. This would result in far more autonomy and direct influence over the whole process for both artists and listeners. It would also reduce the vast disparities of wealth between rich artists and poor artists and between artists and corporate executives.

Let's be very clear here. The advocates of both

neoliberal capitalism and older kinds of free-market liberalism always like to insist that socialism curtails the freedom of individuals. But, in reality, the kinds of system described or proposed here limit only very specific kinds of freedoms for very specific kinds of individuals: the freedom of those who already control capital to pursue further capital accumulation through commodity exchange. The vast majority of people involved in any such socialist system would find their overall power to affect the world in line with their desires to be *increased and enhanced*, not diminished in any way, precisely because they would be able to coordinate with others, making decisions democratically and acting collectively. And that's what 'democracy' actually means.[14]

In an instance such as that of the NHS, there is today very little opportunity for most citizens to involve themselves directly in the management of the service (although, as we will see later, there are good reasons for arguing that this situation should change). But, as a political institution, the NHS is subject to direct and public scrutiny by elected politicians, which is more than could be said of private health providers. More importantly still, the provision of free healthcare to all who need it doesn't simply achieve a decommodification of healthcare for its own sake; it removes one of the major sources of inequality that affect the life chances of modern people. In this, it greatly enhances the capacity of most people to act creatively in the world, either as autonomous persons or as members of groups of any kind. This is always the ultimate aim of socialism.

Liberty, Equality, Solidarity

This is a good example of the way in which socialist policies always try to empower people personally, even as they promote cooperation and higher levels of social equality. In this, the socialist tradition differs fundamentally from those of both liberalism and conservatism. Liberalism believes that we cannot have a society with a higher degree of equality without curtailing the freedom of individuals, and that generally the preservation of individual freedom is more important than the promotion of equality. Liberalism also tends to be suspicious of any attempt to build social solidarity between members of groups and between different groups and communities, assuming that such solidarity can come only by imposing norms and rules on otherwise free individuals. Conservatism, on the other hand, tends to value stability and social solidarity, but agrees with liberalism that these aspects of social life can be sustained only by imposing order from above and by respecting traditional hierarchies of power.

Socialism disagrees with both of these perspectives. Instead, it asserts that the more we are able to build relationships of real solidarity between people, across whatever differences may divide them, while rejecting traditional hierarchies, the more we will be able to create effective democratic institutions that give us the real freedom to create the world we want. From this perspective, there is no trade-off between freedom, equality and solidarity. The three are mutually reinforcing.

As we will see in the chapters to come, one of the challenges faced by socialism in the late twentieth century was the desire for new kinds of personal freedom on the part of millions of people. There is no evidence that this desire has weakened in recent years, especially among the young. Hence it is important to emphasise (and I will) that twenty-first-century socialism is a philosophy and a politics of freedom. But it is also important to remember that, from a socialist perspective, a politics of freedom is always also a politics of equality, solidarity and democracy. This is what socialism has always meant; and it is still what it means today.

Part II

Welcome to the Twenty-First Century

3

How Did We Get Here?

So we've established what we mean by 'capitalism' and 'socialism'. But these are phenomena and ideas that have been around for over two hundred years. The question now is: what are the specific historical circumstances that we all face today? The next two chapters will draw a picture of the contemporary world and explain how we got here, so that we may answer the question about what a twenty-first-century socialism should look like. In this chapter we'll look at the most significant drivers of social, cultural and political change since the mid-twentieth century.

The Cybernetic Revolution

We have been living through a major technological revolution for decades.[1] The development of early

49

computer and electronic technologies was intensively accelerated during the Second World War. In the decades that followed, major innovations such as silicon microchips, user-friendly computer interfaces and computer networking were developed in university departments, corporate research labs and military facilities. By the early 1970s, all the major technical components of modern computing had been invented.[2]

It is debatable whether this represents a historic shift, on the scale of the first Industrial Revolution, or merely one comparable with the second Industrial Revolution of the late nineteenth century – which brought us electrification, the cinema, the radio, powered flight, the internal combustion engine and the telephone. Either way, the consequences have been enormous. Computing, robotics, digital technologies, networking and electronic communications have transformed our social world. All these advances are based on developing 'cybernetic' technologies – that is, on techniques for the communication of information within increasingly complex mechanical systems.[3]

The cybernetic revolution has posed a major problem for the political left. Socialism was born out of the experiences of the first Industrial Revolution and came to political maturity in the wake of the second. The story of modern democratic politics is the story of people learning to adapt to this new world of factories, cities, railways and roads. The first to adapt to these novelties were the capitalists who grew rich from them. For a generation or two, ordinary people could do little but accept their fate: they were driven from the land, herded into hellish factories, forced to work for near-starvation wages. But, over time, they learned to take advantage of their new situation. Crowded together in factories, towns and cities, they formed unions and political parties; they went on strike and demanded the right to vote. They founded political parties, published their own newspapers, set up their own schools. Eventually they formed governments of their own, enacting policies and creating institutions that would transform the lives of their people and those of their descendants.[4]

This history culminated in the middle decades of the twentieth century. In 1930s' America, Roosevelt's government administered a new set of relationships between workers, bosses and government – the New Deal, which laid the foundations for post-war prosperity while containing and regulating capitalist power. In Western Europe and elsewhere, the post-war governments extended the functions of their welfare states to include not just basic services, but the public provision of arts, culture, and higher education.[5] In the Soviet Union, China, and their many satellites, powerful military regimes declared allegiance to the ideals of social- ism and workers' power.

All these achievements were based on the mastery of certain techniques of collaboration, strategy and communication. Organising a union, winning an election, taking over a factory: to do any of these things, you need to deploy certain techniques and use certain technologies. You need to be able to get large numbers of people together in one place at a time – on a shop floor, on a street corner, in a town centre. You need to be able to communicate with them quickly, in large numbers, and in such a way that the bosses can't spy on you or interfere with you. In order to get people organised beyond their local communities, you need to be able to commu- nicate with large numbers of them simultaneously, through postal networks, radio, newspapers, or even television.[6] Once in government, if you want to achieve socialist objectives, you need to be able to do all these things on a national scale; and you also need to be able to control a great deal of what happens within your national borders and at those borders. You need to be able to find out exactly what property rich individuals and corporations hold, so that you may tax them, regulate them or expropriate them. You need to be able to stop them from taking their wealth out of the country.[7]

The cybernetic revolution has made it very difficult to do almost any of that in the ways in which people had learned to do it between the early nineteenth and the mid-twentieth centuries. This is because, once again, capitalists and their corporations got access to the new technologies much earlier than workers and other ordinary citizens did.

Suppose you have a company that manufactures televisions. Before the 1960s, it would have been too costly for such factories to source most of their components far away from the factories where the TV sets themselves were made, or to produce these sets far away from the places where they would be sold. In fact the best way for TV manufacturers to cut costs would be for them to manufacture as much of a TV set as possible in the same place where it would finally be assembled, and then to sell it to local retailers.

The trouble with this arrangement, from a capitalist perspective, is: what happens if some of the workers in your factory decide to go on strike for higher pay? There they all are in the same place, easily able to talk to one another, make plans together, raise demands together. Even if the workers making components are based somewhere else, they are probably nearby; chances are they all belong to the same union, all speak the same language, all share a degree of natural sympathy with one another. The strike is likely to spread and remain solid until the workers get what they want.

The cybernetic revolution makes a neat solution possible. With global computer networking (along with the new developments in containerised shipping), it becomes much easier to situate your factory that makes televisions very far away from the one that makes TV components. The latter might be on an entirely different continent and might be owned by a different company, staffed by workers who have never even heard of the place where your TV factory is located. What is more, your TV factory no longer has to be located anywhere near the place where your TVs are sold, either. If unions are too well organised and workers are too well paid in that place, why not just move the whole factory somewhere more congenial? Besides, if you do that, you might discover that socialist and social–democratic governments in your own country find it much harder to see what you are up to – and harder also to regulate you and to tax you. And if they are still trying. . . well, you could always move your company head office to a country with a lighter tax regime.

How Did We Get Here?

Globalisation and the Postmodern Society

These were the technological conditions underlying the 'globalisation' of the world economy in the late twentieth century.[8] Globalisation is a real phenomenon, as any westerner who uses Chinese-manufactured goods in his or her daily life is aware. But it was also a political project, deliberately engineered and maintained by politicians, business people, corporations, and supra-international institutions like the International Monetary Fund. As a project, globalisation was always intended to weaken the capacity of national governments and national populations to regulate the behaviour of capitalists, tax their profits or interfere with processes of capital accumulation.[9]

By the 1990s, governments led by traditional social–democratic parties – the US Democrats, the British Labour Party, the German Social Democratic Party – claimed that they could no longer implement traditional socialist or social–democratic programmes. If they tried to nationalise industries or regulate capital flows, then companies would simply relocate, investment would dry up, and unemployment would ensue. These claims were always exaggerated, but they were never entirely untrue. Governments such as Tony Blair's never made the slightest effort to find new ways to regulate international capital; but it was true that, if big investors didn't like what a government was doing, they could now remove their investments, leaving the companies that relied on them effectively bankrupt – and this at the speed of an electronic data transfer.

As money and jobs moved around the world, people followed in search of livelihoods and security. Rates of migration increased. Even within national borders, fewer people than ever lived in one place or worked at the same job for decades at a time. The new technologies enabled many factory jobs to be automated. The new jobs that arose in their place were more likely to be in retail, in finance or in the growing sections of the media. They involved managing complex information flows – staffing call centres, talking to customers – rather than executing routinised work on assembly lines. This was a world in which being able to think fast, speak persuasively and hold several ideas in your head at the same time counted for more than physical stamina, sober appearance or reliable punctuality.[10]

Modern industrial societies had encouraged people to become rational, disciplined, dependable, conformist, with a strong belief in progress and the awesome power of science. But these new societies placed a higher value on mobility, flexibility, adaptability and communicative skill. They felt so different from the old industrial societies that commentators thought that they could no longer be described as 'modern' in the old sense. They argued that we were now entering a 'postmodern' world.[11]

The Cultural Revolution

But technology and economics weren't the only drivers of this momentous social and cultural change. Just as the global shipping revolution got underway, just as the new computer technologies were being widely adopted across the corporate sector, the generation of those born after the war was coming to maturity. They had never known the deprivation, hardship and insecurity that many of their parents had. They were better educated, better fed, and had more leisure and access to more entertainment than any previous generation in human history. The conformism, deference, sexism and conservatism that characterised post-war society made little sense to them; so they rebelled against it in many different directions. Some called for a new revolution, dreaming of a world liberated from imperialism, patriarchy and capitalism.[12] Others looked for new ways of being in the world that could feel liberating for individuals but didn't require a social revolution: drugs, therapy, yoga, many kinds of music.[13] Still others just wanted sunnier holidays, better food, more sex and more fun. What emerged was a culture in which a wide diversity of lifestyles was tolerated and accepted to an entirely unprecedented degree.

Above all, people who had been subordinated to the authority of white, straight, elite-class men refused that subordination *en masse*. Black people asserted their right to full citizenship within white-dominated societies, including the right to their own cultural identities and forms of expression.[14] Women made clear that they would no longer accept the subordinate position they had been forced into since time immemorial.[15] One can hardly overestimate what a dramatic shift this represented. Nobody knew, and still nobody knows, exactly what it means to live in a society that does not accept women's subordination as given by God and nature. But most contemporary societies have at least accepted that, in principle, women's subordination cannot be tolerated any longer. The lack of certainty as to what this entails is one reason why contemporary social and cultural life has become so complex. But one thing is certain: any twenty-first-century socialism must embrace feminism and the reality of a cosmopolitan, multicultural world.

As mentioned a little earlier, theorists have called this new world 'postmodern'.[16] This can be a confusing term, but it's also a useful one. To get a handle on it, think of it this way. In the 'modern' world, people felt as if they knew where society was headed. It was headed towards a future in which science and technology would continue to make the world a better place, in which traditional, superstitious beliefs would give way to an enlightened, rational, scientific understanding of processes and phenomena. There were different visions of how to get there, and the Cold War was basically a conflict over whether the best way to create an enlightened, rational society was through free-market American capitalism or through state-directed Soviet-style socialism. But both sides agreed that a scientific, rational society was what they wanted and that humanity was heading towards it. The human story was a story of progress, however you defined it.

Today we live in a world in which some of the most powerful and influential political movements reject the very idea of progress and scientific rationality. This is true of evangelical creationists, hardcore Zionists (who treat the Bible as a legal authority), jihadists, followers of Hindutva and the Iranian Islamic Revolution – but also of many followers of New Age beliefs and of conspiracy theories of all kinds. Even those of us who still basically believe in science are likely to incorporate elements from many different cultures, traditions and belief systems into our daily lives and our views of the world. I know that yoga works for me, even though I have no idea whether there really are currents of mysterious life energy running around my body, as the classic texts of the tantric tradition claim. As for science itself, physicists have not actually been able to agree on the fundamental nature of physical reality for the past hundred years.[17] This is the postmodern world.[18]

No human society on record has come close to accepting the diversity of lifestyle, personal philosophy, religious practice or sexual identity that most of us now regard as normal. This is a challenge that no twenty-first-century socialism can lose sight of. Twentieth-century socialism often promoted a culture of strict conformity in order to foster a sense of unity among the people; in North Korea this model survives even today. A successful twenty-first-century socialism can't be like that. It must be able to mobilise large numbers of people around issues and interests that they have in common, while treating the diversity and plurality of its constituencies as a positive strength, to be welcomed and encouraged. It must find ways for people to make decisions together and act on those decisions without having to agree on everything else.

The Crisis of Democracy

The 'postmodernisation' of culture and society since the 1960s has had significant implications for the way we do politics.[19] The party political system, especially in countries like the United Kingdom and the United States, is still based on the model of mass representative democracy that emerged in the 1920s and 1930s. This was precisely the moment when the technologies of the second Industrial Revolution (broadcasting, cinema, railways, electrification, etc.) were making it possible to mobilise whole national populations, to govern entire countries from a central administration, while generating media and consumer durables for hundreds of thousands of consumers at one time. This produced a situation in which millions of people found themselves living very similar lives: consuming the same media, doing similar jobs in large plants or corporations, engaging in similar pastimes.

Our modern system of representative democracy

emerged along with this 'mass society' and, arguably, made sense under those conditions. That system, based as it is on political parties led by professional politicians, assumes that it's reasonable to expect millions of people at a time to be satisfactorily represented by the same organisation on all issues, for a period of a full four or five years. It assumes that one party will be able to command agreement among millions of voters, on its positions concerning everything – from environmental policy to sports administration. In the postmodern culture of today, this seems ridiculous.[20]

This isn't a new argument. In the 1960s and 1970s, activists and thinkers of the New Left often argued that we should be leaving behind the bureaucratic, top-down administrative systems of the post-war world. They called for systems of local and national government that would enable far more citizens to get actively involved in decision-making; and they spoke in favour of bringing democracy into the management of workplaces, public services and corporations.[21] But little (if any) of this happened.

Instead, since the 1970s, most societies have witnessed a dramatic weakening of their democratic institutions. In both the United States and the United Kingdom, at the end of the long post-war boom the country faced difficult choices as to whether to cut back on public spending, restrain wage growth or accept permanent reductions in capitalist profits. The political right, obviously not favouring the last option, did all it could to spread propaganda that reduced the chance that citizens and governments would take concerted action to limit the power of capital still further. In particular, conservative media, lobbyists and think tanks began to spread the idea that what was needed was significant reductions in wages and welfare spending.[22] At the same time, they encouraged the notion that the growing sense of insecurity and cultural fragmentation could be blamed on disruptive immigrants, crime-prone black people, unworthy welfare recipients, greedy trade unionists, uppity feminists, perverted homosexuals and wild-eyed student hippy radicals. At the end of the 1970s, governments began to be elected on the promise of containing all these unruly elements and of restoring 'law and order'* and a sense of national pride. In fact, what those governments did was to engineer short-term consumer booms while cutting public

---

* In fact this phrase had first been popularised by Richard Nixon in the late 1960s. See Carl Freedman, *The Age of Nixon: A Study in Cultural Power* (London: Zero Books, 2012).

investment and overseeing the transfer of manufacturing jobs to other countries.[23]

The core neoliberal economic programme, to
which most subsequent governments have remained
committed, never commanded widespread popular
support. But, after the catastrophic political defeats
that the left had suffered in the 1980s in societies
in which the media were controlled by capitalists
to an unprecedented degree, it became impossible
to unite public majorities around a coherent alternative agenda. Electoral participation rates fell.
Corporate lobbying became a multibillion-dollar
industry. Almost the only exceptions were in Latin
America.[24]

When Blair's government supported the United
States' invasion of Iraq, defying by far the largest
mass protests in British history, it became apparent both to professional observers and to ordinary
citizens that they were now living in the age
of 'post-democracy'.[25] Under post-democracy, the
rules and rituals of liberal democracy have to be
observed, but the capacity of citizens collectively
to influence the actual activities of governments
is reduced to almost zero. Twenty-first-century
socialism must acknowledge this crisis of our
democratic institutions and build new ones, fit for
the digital age.

How Did We Get Here?

Neoliberal Culture

Since the 1970s, neoliberal assumptions have insinuated themselves into the language and priorities of educational institutions, of popular television, of many aspects of everyday culture. The neoliberal idea that every human being is, or should be, a competitive entrepreneur, constantly trying to build the value of his or her personal brand, is found everywhere, from school policy to reality television and dating websites; but this is a notion that would have seemed strange and repugnant to most people in most cultures at most points in history before the 1980s.[26]

Most people still don't want to be subject to neoliberal norms. They want to make friends because making friends is nice, not just because an extensive network of contacts will give them a competitive advantage in the job market. They want to do a job that feels like it makes the world better, not just one that makes somebody rich. Teachers want to teach and students want to learn because teaching and learning are fundamental to any fulfilled human existence, and not just so that the corporations that students will work for can make more money.

Because people are so reluctant to accept these neoliberal norms, over the past forty years a new class of professional managers has arisen whose primary task is to force or cajole people into accepting them. Their main job, unlike that of old managers of businesses or government agencies, is not to make sure that the organisation runs efficiently and effectively. Their job is instead to discipline other workers within the organisation, to force them to follow neoliberal norms such as meeting targets and fulfilling competitive criteria. A complex and oppressive bureaucracy has grown since the 1970s, in corporations and in the public sector, the purpose of which is to monitor, audit and direct the behaviour of citizens constantly, forcing them to comply with neoliberal codes.[27]

By the end of the 1990s, this new managerial class had taken over not just most major organisations; it had taken over governments and the leadership of most major political parties, creating a professional political elite of politicians, journalists, lobbyists and think-tank 'experts'.[28] Whatever party this elite claimed allegiance to, its real loyalty was to its own social group and to those above it in the social hierarchy (i.e. to capitalists). In the United Kingdom and United States alone, the similarities between the policies of Clinton, Major, Bush, Obama, Blair, Brown and Cameron were more striking than their differences. Almost all of them – from workfare to 'charter' schools and 'academies' – were designed to compel the population to be the best neoliberals they could be.

So why did people put up with it? Why did so many people accept a life they didn't choose, playing by rules they didn't like – rules that every religion and thoughtful philosophy in the history of human culture would have condemned as barbaric? This was partly because there didn't seem to be any other way. In the 1980s, the worldwide labour movement suffered catastrophic defeats, as globalisation and the cybernetic revolution ripped the ground out from under them. The collapse of Soviet communism made it look, to many people, as if the game of history were at an end and the only winner were capitalism.

But it was also because they were being offered lives of unprecedented luxury. Cheap manufactured goods from China, easy consumer credit, inexpensive air travel and the fruits of ongoing technological innovation meant that even the relatively poor could enjoy a lifestyle that once would have been the preserve of the wealthy. This everyday hedonism has become a central feature of life in the twenty-first century, because it is the main compensation we've been offered for the decline of democracy and the unwelcome power of neoliberalism.[29]

Together, the bureaucratic implementation of neoliberalism, the growing precarity of the labour market, and the spread of a culture that values private consumption above all other activities have produced another profound effect that any contemporary socialism must contend with. Today most people have very little regular experience of working effectively in groups with other people. They probably don't know their neighbours. Their co-workers won't be their co-workers long enough for them to get to know one another. Even if they do, what they have in common with their co-workers is probably a 'bullshit job',[30] which none of them wants to be doing and over which they feel no sense of control. In many sectors they may be working on short-term contracts, so their current co-workers will be their competitors in the labour market once the present contract runs out. When they have to attend meetings, those meetings are boring, bureaucratic and frustrating, seeming to prove the neoliberal hypothesis that people acting together can achieve nothing. They fill their hours with social media, communicating with people most of whom they will never meet and with whom they will almost never do anything more substantial than share memes. They find pleasure and satisfaction in their private lives, as consumers, on holiday, maybe pursuing solitary hobbies,[31] probably just watching television.

Neoliberalism says that people are happier this way – consuming, competing, pursuing their private interests. They are not. They use platform technologies and a vast range of drugs to try to make themselves feel better, to feel some connection with other people and the wider world. But this experience of daily life often makes it feel to them as if actually getting things done with other people is impossible, especially if those things have any objective other than making money. If socialism in the twenty-first century has a single objective, that objective is to turn people's desire for connection into real social and cooperative action for the greater good.[32] And, if it has a single obstacle to overcome, then it is the feeling that no such thing is possible – a feeling that the whole machinery of neoliberal culture deliberately inculcates in people.

4

Where Are We Now?

In this chapter we'll look at the most pressing social problems of our time that follow on from the major shifts discussed in chapter 3.

Climate Crisis

Climate change poses an unprecedented challenge to human civilisation.[1] Global warming is caused by the fact that too much carbon dioxide is released into the atmosphere, almost entirely through the burning of fossil fuels. Fossil fuels are burned to release energy, which is in turn used to produce commodities, to move commodities and workers around, and to power appliances.

It may be possible to find technical solutions that allow us to go on doing all this without emitting carbon dioxide, CO_2.[2] But presently, although research into renewable energy has made huge strides in recent decades, the current levels of investment and research going into developing these technologies are nowhere close to what would be required to make this a realistic prospect. Only far more investment in this endeavour will make it even plausible that effective technical solutions can be found and applied on a global scale. Corporations are not going to make this investment, because it is not profitable. Only if a considerable proportion of the energy, labour and resources that are currently devoted to the goal of generating profits for corporations is redirected towards the objective of developing and applying green technologies – only on that condition will there be hope for a technological solution. Without international coordination and determined action on the part of governments that are committed to reducing the power of capitalism, there is no way this is going to happen.

The best science tells us that, without urgent action, climate change will reach a point of catastrophic irreversibility within twelve years.[3] Technological solutions cannot be implemented that quickly. But not many experts believe that a technological shift alone will ever be able to resolve the crisis. In both the short term and the long term, addressing the crisis will mean changing the way we live, so that, at the very least, we produce less stuff. At the most extreme, we may have to travel less (or at least travel very differently) and live lives that require less power consumption overall.

This is not to say that addressing the climate crisis requires us to adopt lifestyles that are any less luxurious than our present ones. It means that production needs to be reoriented towards more durable rather than more profitable commodities: better quality clothes, more durable devices, better insulated homes. It means reorienting food production towards practices such as sustainable farming (which makes food taste better anyway). All this would cut into capitalist profits. None of it would mean less pleasant lives for us.

But none of this is going to be possible without a very high level of social organisation and coordination, of a kind that is simply not obtainable in a society that lets the market decide how to distribute all its resources. Such coordination might well be undertaken by authoritarian governments, which would impose strict rules on corporations, institutions and individuals; or it might be undertaken democratically, through the large-scale voluntary mobilisation of whole populations. Obviously the latter would be preferable, and likely to prove more effective: people are more willing to accept a change to their lifestyles if they have been involved in making the necessary decisions about what has to change and how it will.

The ecological emergency makes socialism more necessary than ever. It also means that a twenty-first-century socialism must have a strong international dimension, looking beyond the power of individual nation-states to regulate their own economies and seeking to build up international institutions and alliances on a scale that could make it possible to tackle the climate crisis. Within specific countries, it must seek to develop institutions that enable entire populations to discuss, deliberate and make decisions on the most fundamental questions facing us as a species. Otherwise it will never be able to overcome the propaganda of capitalists, who are sure to keep offering easy solutions and downright lies in order to keep shoring up their profits.[4]

The Changing World of Work

In the nineteenth century Marx predicted that, as capital became concentrated in the hands of a tiny elite, the vast majority of people would find themselves forced to join the proletariat – the working class that can only survive by selling its labour. Eventually the proletariat would be large enough to overwhelm the power of the capitalist class (*la bourgeoisie* – literally 'the suburban class' in French). Socialist revolution would follow. The middle classes – the petit bourgeois owners of small businesses, professionals such as teachers, doctors and lawyers – were expected to dwindle into insignificance; and that was no bad thing, given that they were incorrigibly and permanently reactionary.[5]

Some of this turned out to be accurate. Actual ownership of capital has concentrated on a global scale. In the 1930s, the petite bourgeoisie was the social group most likely to support fascism. Most professionals today are not self-employed entrepreneurs, as they were in Marx's time, but salaried workers with relatively little access to real wealth. Consequently, in countries such as the United Kingdom, entire professions (teaching, medicine) are no longer part of the traditional petite bourgeoisie, but form a subclass of more or less well paid, highly educated, highly organised workers whose natural political sympathies are to the left.

In other ways, things have not gone according to Marx's plan. In countries such as the United States and the United Kingdom, the industrial working class, which was the traditional base for socialist and labour politics, has been dwindling for decades. At the same time, affluent workers have become homeowners and pension holders in large numbers, and these positions give them access to some of the direct benefits of capital ownership.

Most dramatically, the petite bourgeoisie has not continued to contract (although it did so until the 1960s). Today far more people are self-employed in the private sector or work for small to medium-sized businesses than was the case forty years ago.[6] The middle classes are a larger, more variegated collection of subgroups (or class fractions) than ever before, and they have complex sets of political and cultural allegiances.[7] The traditional petite bourgeoisie of medium-sized business owners and of corporate middle management remains the bedrock of political reaction, being more likely than any other social group – apart from the wealthiest 1 per cent – to have voted for Trump or for Brexit. But public sector professionals constitute a distinctive group that shares absolutely nothing with them, despite also being characterised as 'middle class': teachers, for example, are more likely than almost any other social group to be members of trade unions and to vote for left-wing parties.[8]

Most importantly, we have seen the emergence of what one might call the 'new petite bourgeoisie' of entrepreneurs and freelancers – especially in the technology and media sectors. They have a historically distinctive culture and highly fluid political allegiances. They place a high value on personal freedom and on the ability to pick and choose between isolated parts of different cultures that appeal to them: they listen to reggae in the car, but certainly do not embrace Rastafarianism; they do yoga on a Saturday, but certainly do not become tantric devotees; they get married in traditional style because they find the ceremony picturesque, but never go to church again, and so on.[9] They tend to be culturally individualistic, but also to rely heavily on public services, especially if they have families. They liked Thatcher's and Reagan's celebrations of entrepreneurial culture but disliked their nationalism, their warmongering, their emphasis on traditional 'family values'. They were enthusiastic about Blair and Clinton during the heady days of the 1990s' tech boom, but today they are probably very worried about climate change and aware that governments allied with big business are unlikely to do anything about it. They tend to avoid joining unions, and any political rhetoric that seems to be 'anti-business' will be anathema to them. But they are probably sympathetic to attempts to limit the power of banks and major corporations, as long as smaller businesses are seen to be supported and valued. Perhaps they like the idea of belonging to a coop, although they almost certainly don't. They *love* their computers, their smartphones and their social media platforms.

Today this is a crucial constituency for social-ists to win support from. And winning it is by no means impossible, despite these people's lack of affinity with the tradition of organised labour. Twenty-first-century socialism can appeal to their sense of modernity, their mistrust of corporate con-servatism, their dislike of hierarchy and their love of comfort. These are all qualities that members of the new petite bourgeoisie share with many other sections of society: insecure graduates, public sector workers, and indeed all but the most conservative sections of the working class.

I have focused on the new petite bourgeoisie because I think this is the social constituency that is up for grabs more than any other. Such people could be won over by a twenty-first-century socialism; but socialism doesn't have the same spontaneous appeal for them as it does for public sector workers and insecure workers in the private sector. It's these latter groups that already represent the core base of electoral support for politicians such as Bernie Sanders, Alexandria Ocasio-Cortez and Jeremy

Corbyn. They, too, face a distinctive set of challenges, of course. Public sector workers have been in the front line of the struggle against neoliberalism for decades, because neoliberalism promotes the contraction and privatisation of public services, while imposing a rigid, punitive bureaucracy in the public sector.[10] Above all, the changes we have been discussing in this book – globalisation, the cybernetic revolution, neoliberalism, and so on – have created a situation in which many workers now find themselves living from month to month, without guaranteed long-term income, without adequate benefits or pension provision. Corporations don't want to hire people for longer than necessary in a highly fluid economy. Unions are difficult to organise in such a complex and mobile world. The result is a situation in which general insecurity or 'precarity' (i.e. precarious living in unpredictable economic circumstances) is a common experience shared by both the poorest workers and many graduates who would once have expected to enjoy the secure prosperity of the established middle class.

The final change to the world of work for us to consider here is potentially the most devastating, if also the simplest to understand. The latest stage of the cybernetic revolution threatens to see a huge proportion of the jobs currently done by humans being automated out of existence, as 'artificial intelligence' and 'machine learning' (basically, computers doing routine tasks very quickly) increase the capacity of computers to do everything, from routine medical diagnosis to most forms of advanced accounting. The question of whether this will lead to greater amounts of free time for everyone or to a vast increase in the rate of unemployment remains an open one.[11]

Despite these many changes to the nature and distribution of work in the twenty-first century, one fact has not changed at all. In countries such as the United Kingdom, where unions and social–democratic institutions have been most severely weakened by neoliberalism, the amount of hours put in by workers per week, on average, has barely changed since the 1990s.[12] At the same time, many workers find themselves either forced to work far longer hours than they want to or unable to find enough regular employment to pay the bills. The steady decline in average working hours, from around 60 hours per week in the nineteenth century to less than 40 by the 1970s, was the most obvious and measurable indicator of progress for working people during that entire period. If anything can be taken to demonstrate that such progress has been halted during the neoliberal era, as the power of capital has been restored, then it is this: the proportion of their lives that most people are forced to consecrate to work in order to maintain an acceptable standard of living has stopped shrinking – although, of course, this is not the case in those Western European and Scandinavian countries where social–democratic institutions remain stronger.

Platform Capitalism

As the twentieth century drew to a close, it was possible for almost all those who were working in fields such as new media and information technology to see themselves as surfing the same revolutionary wave. From the web page designer working for coffee to the CEO of the bedroom dotcom start-up, nobody knew exactly where the cybernetic revolution was heading and everyone had a chance to get rich.[13]

Now we know where it was heading. It was heading towards a place in which a tiny number of techno-capitalists would get incredibly, unbelievably rich, while life for most other people would get much harder. It was heading to a place in which a handful of enormous corporations – Google, Facebook, Amazon, YouTube, Apple – would come to dominate global culture, accumulating billions as they turned the Internet into a far more homogenous space than it was once supposed to be. It was heading towards a future in which every social interaction would be monitored and monetised as a piece of resellable data by the owners of the platform on which it occurred. Welcome to the world of platform capitalism.[14]

Platform capitalism marks the second stage of the cybernetic revolution. The first stage brought us mainframe computing, electronic networking and the first appearance of the World Wide Web. This new phase has seen the Internet become integral to everyday life, media culture and global commerce. The corporations that have been able to make billions in this context are those able to profit from the vast aggregations of people and data that occur on multiuser online platforms. For the most part, they don't actually produce anything; as is so typical of capitalism throughout its history, the big money accrues to the middlemen. What they provide is platforms that connect millions of users or websites with one another, or millions of customers with retailers. Google and Facebook make their money almost entirely from collecting data on the behaviour of their users and selling them back to advertisers.[15]

This has created a world of new political possibilities. On the right, shady consultancies have used data analytics to target propaganda at voters, nudging them towards support for Brexit or for Trump.[16] On the left, the election of Jeremy Corbyn as Labour leader would not have been likely to happen without Facebook groups that enabled his supporters to get a sense of how large their numbers actually were.[17] These are just two examples out of many of how a mass movement was enabled by the creative use of social media.[18]

Platform apps have been used to spread right-wing conspiracy theories;[19] they've also been used as essential organising tools by progressive campaigners. But, despite this apparent flexibility, the platforms that have become central to contemporary culture are all vast private monopolies, unaccountable to anyone but their shareholders. In this context, the question of who has access to data about people, to flows of information of all kinds, to software and to network infrastructure, becomes a central political question. Any contemporary socialism will have to address it as more than just a peripheral concern, as well as figuring out how to use platform technologies to advance socialism rather than simply to accumulate profits.

Perhaps more immediately, the growth of platform capitalism presents an extraordinary threat to basic human freedom. Platform corporations generate most of their profits by harvesting data from users, collecting information about their movements, preferences, thoughts and feelings through the careful monitoring of locations, messages, purchases, posts and responses to posts. In most countries this activity is currently subject to almost no effective legal oversight, because the existing legal frameworks were not developed to accommodate such technological capacities. Almost all our social activity is treated by these companies as an opportunity to generate profit; and they do this by monitoring our behaviour and selling the information to advertisers.[20] In the process they are building up a more complete and intrusive database of information on us than any government has ever held on its people. This is the nature of what Zuboff calls 'surveillance capitalism'. But we have no access to those data, no control over them, and we do not benefit from them materially, even though it is we who generate them.

Here is a major imbalance of power, to be corrected in the twenty-first century. The solution to this problem cannot be merely legal. Governments could regulate these companies, introduce laws to protect our privacy, break up platform monopolies;

but this would only slow down their activities, not put a halt to them or redirect them altogether. This is because what drives this behaviour from corporations is not something inherent in platform technologies themselves. Rather it is something inherent in capitalism: the relentless drive for unlimited accumulation. In the end, if we want to limit or even halt the endless surveillance, the only way to do it will be to take these technologies out of the hands of capitalists altogether.

After the Crash

The 2008 financial crisis saw a number of major financial institutions (banks, investment firms) go bankrupt, while many others had to be supplied with enormous injections of cash by governments: cash that those governments had to borrow and are still nowhere close to repaying.[21] The causes of the crisis were complex and need not detain us here for long. But, in a nutshell, banks had been lending money to people who would never be able to afford to pay it back, and the international finance system had become so complex that nobody was exactly clear which banks were owed how much money by how many of these people who could never pay it back. Once this became apparent, almost every bank and investment company in the world panicked, refusing to lend money to one another in case the company they lent it to was about to go bankrupt. The global system of finance, borrowing and investment almost entirely seized up.[22]

Governments could have simply nationalised the banks, as they did in the 1930s and 1940s, stabilising the system: but, to do that successfully, they would have had to deprive the banks' shareholders and creditors of billions in assets and expected profits. The international neoliberal political elite had been brought into existence for no other reason than to serve the interests of those shareholders; they were not about to seize their assets now. Instead, they allowed their governments to borrow vast sums of money, which they then handed over to the banks, telling them to plug their own financial holes with it. It is because those governments are still repaying those loans that government investment in public services, in manufacturing infrastructure and in scientific research has all been drastically cut in recent years. This is the origin of contemporary austerity.[23]

Austerity has drastic knock-on effects on the overall economy. Reduced government spending and investment means fewer public sector jobs, hence fewer customers for companies that might sell things to public sector workers. It also means fewer government contracts for various companies that supply the public sector. That means in turn significantly fewer opportunities for companies across the private sector. Reduced welfare entitlements, cuts in training and education budgets for young people, all mean that many workers – especially young ones – are forced to work for much lower wages than they otherwise would have done. The result has been the most dramatic fall in real terms wages since the Industrial Revolution.[24] In these circumstances, many people have not been able to spend and consume to the extent they'd become accustomed to during the 1980s, 1990s and the decade 2000–10.

For this reason, the past decade has seen the political elite gradually lose its authority, as fewer and fewer people have been offered the compensation of high levels of consumption in return for the contraction of public services, rising inequality, and the weakening of democracy itself. So people have rejected the politics, culture and authority of the professional political class in many different ways. Some have rejected it by voting for authoritarian, right-wing political programmes that disdain the cosmopolitan culture of the political elite, holding out the illusory promise of a restored a sense of national pride and purpose. This is the basis for votes in favour of Brexit and Trump. Others have rejected it by supporting candidates and political projects that promise to break with the decades of neoliberal rule, to pursue a socialist programme and to transform the institutions government. This has been the basis for the rise in support for Podemos in Spain, for Jeremy Corbyn's Labour Party in the United Kingdom and for Bernie Sanders in the United States, as well as for small left-wing parties in many other countries.

In the United States and the United Kingdom, despite a marked shift to the left among young voters[25] and an almost total collapse of support for the political elite, the fact that neoliberal ideas and practices are so deeply entrenched in public and private institutions, in the media and in everyday culture still presents a huge challenge to any progressive political project. In the United Kingdom, supporters of Jeremy Corbyn experience enormous frustration at the flagrant hostility shown towards him by most political journalists. This is not surprising. Corbyn's rise to prominence is a direct effect of the public's rejecting the authority of the professional political class that those journalists belong to.

At the same time, the content of much other media output is saturated by neoliberal ideology: the endless, ritualised competitions that constitute the output of much 'reality' television, for example.[26] The implicit message of so much of that output is to reinforce neoliberal assumptions about the nature of human beings and the social world. The question of how to challenge such assumptions, both in practice and in theory, is one that any twenty-first-century socialism must confront.

Culture War

As well as challenging such persistent neoliberal assumptions, any radical politics today must face the resurgence of authoritarian, conservative, and nationalistic ideologies, as personified by Trump, Erdogan, Modi and Bolsonaro. These political tendencies have grown and spread around the world, largely in reaction to the combined social and cultural effects of neoliberalism, globalisation and cultural revolution. In particular, they have tended to be popular among people who feel that they have nothing to gain from the consequence of that revolution. This category includes two main groups. One consists of wealthy straight white men, who have seen their authority only eroded by the cultural revolution. On the other hand, it includes some very poor people, who just don't have the money to be able to participate easily in postmodern consumer culture.

Poor, uneducated people are not stupid. But by definition they have access to fewer and less reliable channels of information than other people. It takes a lot resources to reach them and give them information. And who has those resources? The rich white guys. It's not an accident that the first of the modern right-wing populist leaders was Silvio Berlusconi – prime minister of Italy several times between 1986 and 2017 and billionaire owner of a large chunk of Italy's media. And, so, rich white men like Berlusconi (or Rupert Murdoch, or Donald Trump) use their resources to tell poor people a story.

That story has to explain the sense of displacement and disempowerment experienced by poor and uneducated people under conditions of globalisation and neoliberalism. But obviously it cannot explain that most of those problems are caused by capitalists and their relentless quest for profit. So, according to that story, it's instead immigrants, feminists, foreigners, LGBTQ people and cosmopolitan liberals who are the cause of the problems.

Today the bloggers, YouTubers and meme artists of the alt-right use platform technologies to circulate, amplify and embellish such beliefs for audiences of millions. Explicitly challenging this narrative is a key task for any progressive movement today.

The Rent's Too High

The platform corporations didn't rise to prominence all by themselves. Silicon Valley has worked hand in glove with some of the oldest and most powerful forces of global capitalism: the banks and financial institutions of Wall Street. The tech industry has relied on huge levels of speculative investment for its growth, while the growing power of finance since the 1970s has been fed by information and communication technologies, without which everything from credit cards to high-frequency stock-market trading would be impossible.

Unlike the tech industry or manufacturing, finance doesn't do anything useful. It doesn't make or invent anything. All it does is to move money around, lending it and borrowing it, placing bets on which shares and currencies will rise or fall in value over a given period. And yet, during the period of neoliberalism, there has been growing pressure on all kinds of business, including those that do make and invent useful things, to behave in the same way: to seek short-term profits, to work towards maximising their share price by any means available, to invest in other companies for purely speculative reasons. This process of financialisation has been intimately bound up with the neoliberal programme, because neoliberal policies have been enacted only in those places where finance capitalists and their close allies were at their most powerful.[27]

Among those allies, the most important are landlords and real estate developers. Financialisation involves an endless quest for profits through the trading of assets and the monopolisation of resources, without actually creating anything new. Economists sometimes call this search for profits without the actual production of anything useful 'rent seeking'. Rent seeking is also, literally, what landlords do, and in fact real estate developers, speculators and landlords are often also bankers and traders in shares or currencies. The deregulation of financial markets since the 1960s has been accompanied in many places by the deregulation of property markets, which has removed legal and financial protections from renters and encouraged citizens to take out mortgages, in an effort to become property owners themselves (while generating huge profits for banks).

The consequence of this process is that many cities are becoming places in which ordinary people cannot afford to live. Property prices are too high for people to buy homes, as a result of the number of wealthy investors purchasing properties as speculative investments. Then people are forced to rent; in consequence, the demand for rented accommodation rises. Rents are too high, because there is not enough rented accommodation to meet the demand and because municipal governments have not invested in social housing, which is the best way to lower the demand for private rentals. The result is a seemingly never-ending inflation of property values. In recent decades, the reality of young people tending to be 'priced out' of the housing market, while their parents see the market value of their homes increase exponentially, has led to a growing sense of frustration among the young that has fuelled some of the most impressive protests against the neoliberal order – from the Indignados movement in Spain to the Occupy movement in the United States and to the waves of support for Bernie Sanders and Jeremy Corbyn.[28]

But it is not only the young who suffer. As cities are transformed from living communities into three-dimensional investment portfolios for the rich, their culture and social fabric inevitably deteriorate. Local arts and culture decline, because nobody can afford rehearsal or studio space; venues close and community spaces contract. This is happening in cities all over the world. Socialism began life in the industrial cities. It is and always will be an urban movement. That doesn't mean that it offers benefits only to city dwellers; far from it. But socialism cannot allow the cities to be captured by capitalists; and socialism is the only way to reclaim the cities from them.

These, then, are the specific conditions under which all politics takes place today: climate change, the cybernetic revolution, globalisation, changes to the class structure, the crisis of representative democracy, the reality of postmodern culture, the rise of platform capitalism, the legacy of neoliberalism, the resurgence of the authoritarian right and the capitalist capture of the cities. All these are factors that any twenty-first century-socialism will have to take into account. In the chapters that follow I will consider some of the historical lessons that it might draw on and what its programs and strategy might actually look like.

Part III

Twenty-First Century Socialism

5

The Programme

So what kind of policies would a twenty-first-century socialism seek to enact, were it able to acquire enough influence within government or state structures?

Any contemporary socialism must be able to respond to the climate crisis, to the conditions created by the cybernetic revolution and globalisation, to the cultural revolution that has produced our postmodern world and to the effects of neoliberal power. It must confront, in the shape of the platform corporations, the largest concentration of capital the world has ever seen.

All this has several implications. Contemporary socialism cannot be authoritarian in nature, relying on a culture of conformity, as twentieth-century socialism so often did. After the cultural revolution, this just isn't going to work. At the same time, in every zone of social life that neoliberalism has tried to turn into a competitive marketplace, socialism must instead promote creative cooperation and democracy. Recognising the crisis of liberal representative democracy, it must embrace the idea of more participatory, inclusive, deliberative and continuous forms of democracy in many institutional contexts.[1] It must enable people to work with one another in groups – in their communities, in their workplaces, and in many other situations – and to experience that collaboration as both empowering and liberating.[2] Nor can it expect that those groups will all be confined to neighbourhoods and workplaces. In the digital universe many people feel more attached to their online networks than to their organic ones. Sometimes this can be a problem, but it can also create extraordinary opportunities for large distributed networks of people to act together.[3]

A Genealogy of the Future

The argument that socialism should promote democratic and cooperative institutions – eschewing top-down, hierarchical models – is hardly a new one. In the nineteenth century, this was the basic animating idea of the anarchist wing of the international socialist movement, led by Mikhail Bakunin.[4] Non-revolutionary socialism, too, had powerful democratic currents from its earliest days, as partisans of the cooperative movement and of guild socialism imagined a socialist society as a federation of autonomous, self-organised communities of workers.[5] This idea probably found its fullest expression in post-war Yugoslavia, which implemented a system of 'workers' self-management' whereby most citizens worked as members of relatively autonomous, democratically managed cooperative enterprises rather than in the state-directed factories and farms of the Soviet system.[6]

In Yugoslavia as elsewhere, one of the main problems facing a socialist economy was how to decide what to produce and how much of it, without relying on market competition and without an unconstrained profit motive to discipline retailers and manufacturers. A tantalising yet possible solution was put forward by one of the most innovative governments of the twentieth century. Since the nineteenth century, Latin America has seen revolutionary socialist experiments come and go, alternating with liberal governments, military dictatorships, and many other types of regime. In 1970 Chile – then the most advanced economy of the region – saw an unprecedented occurrence: the election, in free, conventional elections, of an openly Marxist socialist government led by President Salvador Allende. The Allende government famously recruited the British cybernetics expert Stafford Beer to design and start to build a national computer network – Cybersyn, an early Internet – in order to harness the power of network computing and enable citizens around the country to contribute information and requests and thereby facilitate democratic economic planning.[7] But this experiment was never allowed to come to fruition.

The Allende government planned to nationalise assets that belonged to predatory American corporations, and its model of futuristic, democratic socialism was terrifying to the capitalist class and its imperial allies in the US military–industrial complex. The CIA supported, funded and instigated a military coup against the government, installing General Augustus Pinochet, who became one of the most brutal dictators of the late twentieth century for the next seventeen years. They also installed a team of economists from the University of Chicago at the heart of Pinochet's government, allowing them to implement the first fully neoliberal economic programme to be actually enacted – all under the auspices of Pinochet's military government.[8]

The Programme

The global neoliberal programme began with the violent suppression of democratic, technologically sophisticated socialism.

One experiment in democratic, cooperative socialism that has not proven so vulnerable to external threats is the Mondragon corporation. This vast federation of cooperative, worker-owned enterprises and training institutes was founded in the Basque Country in the late 1950s, and today employs over 70,000 people in factories, retail outlets, banking, insurance and a university, all spread across several countries.[9] It is not a socialist institution in the sense of seeking to abolish all capitalist social relations, and it necessarily competes with capitalist corporations in the various sectors in which it operates.[10] But, by not pursuing unlimited accumulation and by working to displace markets actors in those sectors that do, it is strategically anti-capitalist in very significant ways. It is also widely admired as a model of democratic, participatory and cooperative organisation of productive activity and has been an inspiration for initiatives such as Cooperation Jackson in Jackson, Mississippi. This extraordinary project looks to build a 'solidarity economy' and an 'economic democracy' among mainly African American citizens and aims to achieve a network of worker-owned cooperatives as the basis for a real democratic empowerment of some of the poorest people in America (see https:// cooperationjackson.org).

This history provides us with invaluable lessons to draw on as we imagine what a twenty-first-century socialism might consist of. In the final chapter I will consider what kind of political strategies twenty-first-century socialism might deploy to achieve its goals. But first we should ask in more detail what those goals are. What follows is, effectively, a list of policies that a putative socialist government might enact in a country like the United Kingdom or the United States. Whether getting governments elected and getting them to do things is actually likely to be the best way to do twenty-first-century socialism is a whole other question. But there's great value in having a clear idea of what we would ideally like a progressive government to do if we could have one.

Green Socialism

The ultimate aim of any programme for twenty-first-century socialism would be twofold. It would be in part to weaken the power of capitalists fundamentally. It would also be, conversely, to enhance the power of the people, as citizen and as workers.

But, before addressing these long-term objectives, twenty-first-century socialism would have to deal with the most immediate problem facing our societies: the climate crisis.

The idea of a Green New Deal has become central to many current ways of imagining progressive futures, and for very good reasons.[11] The phrase makes a deliberate allusion to Roosevelt's 1930s New Deal programme, which responded to the crisis of the Great Depression with a wholesale reorganisation of the relationships between capitalists, workers and governments and with a vast programme of public works designed to modernise America's industrial infrastructure. Today we need governments to take a lead in organising the transition to a system of energy production, transportation, city planning and manufacturing that would produce very low or zero carbon emissions, while linking this aim to a broader programme of social justice, welfare reform and wealth redistribution.

At the same time, the ecological crisis cannot be addressed without a major rethink of the way in which urban, rural and suburban space are organised and deployed in our societies. A society that depends on motor transport will never be ecologically viable, even if cars are 100 per cent electrified. There is a dire need for rewilding and reforestation of much of the Earth's surface area in order for excess CO_2 to be absorbed from the atmosphere.[12] Hence the twentieth-century model of suburban sprawl facilitated by widespread car use must be abandoned. More and more people will have to live together in cities;[13] so cities must be made livable, affordable and accessible. Crucially, they must be affordable and accessible to the millions of people who will *not* live in them, but will still want to visit them and enjoy their cultural and social riches when the opportunity allows.

The 'right to the city' is something that radicals have called for since the 1960s.[14] This phrase refers to the idea that the city should not become a wholly commodified and privatised set of spaces, segregated by class, mostly accessible to the rich and experienced by others as merely alienating and atomising. Such a right must be seen as integral to any project for an ecological and democratic twenty-first-century socialism.

Weakening the Capitalists, Empowering the People

So what would the rest of a twenty-first-century socialist programme look like? Weakening the power of capitalists would require a number of measures, which involve both the regulation and control of existing capitalist institutions and the creation and empowerment of new, socialist alternatives. One obvious way to reduce the power of finance capital over the rest of society would be to create institutions such as local and national investment banks that could invest in and support new and small businesses, which would no longer be reliant on private loans and investments; this would deprive financial institutions of their exclusive control over the allocation of capital and investment.[15] Another way would be to take back into public ownership many of the services and institutions that have been privatised during the neoliberal era, from railways in the United Kingdom to refuse services in American municipalities.

But what would mark out a twenty-first-century version of this policy by comparison with the social–democratic policies followed in many countries during the mid-twentieth century would be much stronger efforts to ensure that citizens and workers are directly engaged in the democratic management of such institutions.[16] This is not just because the socialist and anarchist traditions have always dreamed of creating democratic institutions of this type. It is because the cultural revolution of the 1960s and 1970s was, as much as anything, a revolt against the paternalistic and bureaucratic culture of the welfare state; and there is no evidence today that large numbers of people want to go back to that. Democratising the public sector is not just a nice idea. It is a political necessity for any form of socialism that wants to win widespread political support.[17]

What would democratising the public sector look like in practice? One example would be for state schools to be offered the opportunity to escape the strictures imposed on them by forty years of neoliberal policy and to become real democratic assets for their communities of users and staff. They should all have the opportunity to be democratic community schools run by staff, students, parents and representatives of the local community, in the interest of helping children to become fulfilled, functioning democratic citizens. Fielding and Moss call this ideal 'the common school'.[18] Neoliberal 'reform' measures, such as school league tables (which publicly rank schools according to the performance of students in standardised tests) should be abolished.[19] All empirical evidence shows that such measures do nothing to improve the education of students.[20]

Extending the reach of the public sector as well

as democratising it is another way to reduce the power that employers and retailers have over so much of our lives. Developing the principle of universal basic services (UBS)[21] would directly reverse the neoliberal trend towards the commodification of everything. The idea behind UBS is to decommodify many areas of social life by extending such services not just to education and healthcare but to transport, energy, communications, and potentially many other areas (e.g. to services that provide access to arts and culture). This is a classic social–democratic principle that has operated successfully in many contexts since the early twentieth century, empowering people personally while reducing the power of capitalists. Today it retains a radical potential to move us away from the neoliberal idea that public services should be organised as if they were profit-making businesses.

Democratic socialist government would also actively seek to encourage cooperative models of ownership and control of enterprises outside of the public sector, as well as the socialisation of enterprises and services at local, municipal and national levels where this is appropriate.[22] One interesting example of such encouragement has been seen in the community wealth-building programmes pursued by municipal governments in cities such as Cleveland, Ohio and Preston, England, which have preferred small local companies, cooperatives in particular, to international corporations when awarding municipal contracts.[23] A very good example of private companies that should be compulsorily socialised is that of the behemoths of platform capitalism. A clear feature of platform economy is that the major platforms in every sector are natural monopolies.[24] So all these corporations should be transitioned into giant 'platform cooperatives'[25] owned by their own users, and the ultimate governing bodies overseeing them should be elected by those users. Their current owners could be generously compensated, but progressive governments should make immediate plans to force this transition upon them. Of course, this would require international cooperation from a network of progressive governments; but so will almost any form of social progress in the networked, globalised world of the twenty-first century.

And, of course, the principle of participatory democracy must be extended into the sphere of government itself. Socialism cannot be built just by electing the right people to office within the existing structures of liberal representative democracy. Twenty-first-century socialism must create the institutional conditions for the emergence of new kinds of meaningful collective self-organisation on multiple scales, from local neighbourhoods to international networks. Democracy should be regarded as the unending process of trying to make that possible and overcoming all limitations on it.[26] At the level of the existing institutions of formal democracy. this would have to involve an ongoing, open-ended and highly ambitious process of democratic reform.[27]

The World of Work

The measures proposed thus far would give communities of citizens far more power than they currently enjoy over public services, elements of the economy, and the institutions of the state. But this could ultimately leave perhaps the most important area of social life entirely controlled by capitalist power: the world of work. In fact, the historical record suggests that none of these measures is likely to be achievable merely through the political efforts of left-wing parties and governments.

If the ability of capitalists to dictate terms to the rest of society is to be challenged, people must be organised not only in their local communities and political parties but in their workplaces, with their fellow workers. Even with left-wing governments in office, there is a great deal that capitalists can do to disrupt the efforts of those governments to implement reforms: closing factories, funding right-wing media, evading their taxes.[28] Historically, the thing that makes them least likely to take such measures is the threat of sustained strike action eating into their profits.

Therefore the active encouragement of trade union membership would be a crucial objective for any twenty-first-century socialist movement or government. Organised labour has been a crucial counterweight to capitalist power since the nineteenth century: without it, neither mass suffrage nor any of the socio-economic reforms of the twentieth century would have been possible. Unions and workers need all the help they can get organising in a world in which capitalist production has been globalised and precarious work has become the norm for so many.[29] Twenty-first-century socialist governments must give them that help by actively using the resources of the state to help them recruit members, publicly stating that union membership is good for people and good for society. They should also do everything they can to coordinate unions and facilitate their finding ways to organise at an international level.

At the same time, simply winning power in

workplaces will not liberate citizens or workers from the sheer brute necessity of work itself, or restore the historic trend towards the reduction of working hours that was the surest sign of social progress over the whole course of the twentieth century. Plans to reduce the working week and to redistribute work and free time equitably across the working population must be a priority for any progressive government. And, crucially, 'work' must be understood to involve currently unpaid work such as childcare and eldercare.[30] One way to achieve such objectives is through the intensive deployment of automative technologies that reduce the amount of human labour required to do all kinds of things, from cleaning homes to complex surgery. But if such policies are enacted in a situation where capitalist power is unchecked, then capitalists will simply use these technologies to reduce their workforce, lowering the overall demand for labour and therefore the wages of other workers. Automation can be of benefit to all only if it is deployed under the supervision of socialist governments, in collaboration with strong trade unions.[31]

Another way to redistribute and reduce workloads is to make all citizens less dependent on work for survival. An extensive programme of free public services is key to achieving this, but, as long as we live in a market economy at all, this method will always have limited effects: people will need money to purchase commodities and will be disenfranchised if they lack it. One way of addressing this problem is with a parallel policy of universal basic income (UBI) – that is, by simply granting all citizens, unconditionally, a certain allowance of spendable income.[32]

Countering Capitalist Lies

Finally, any progressive government and movement today must recognise the extent to which it will be challenged by right-wing propaganda. This will take the form both of explicitly racist, xenophobic and reactionary narratives promoted by conservative media and of the subtler propagation of neoliberal, individualist and pro-capitalist ideas and norms by the more 'liberal' sections of the entertainment industry. Various measures will be required to tackle this situation, from the democratisation of state broadcasters[33] to measures forcing major media corporations to become self-governing trusts, with a remit not to pursue capital accumulation beyond the level necessary to maintain themselves and pay their staff. It should simply not be regarded as a reasonable situation, in any contemporary democracy, that the major organs of the fourth estate are controlled by private individuals or profit-seeking corporations.[34] At the same time, as the media analyst Dan Hind has argued,[35] the media will not be truly democratic unless there are vehicles by which members of the public can influence the actual commissioning of media content. In the twenty-first century it should be perfectly possible to design systems that would make that happen (for example, by enabling members of the public to propose and vote online for news stories to be investigated) – provided that the necessary resources are allocated.

No doubt the programme that I have sketched here leaves out many issues and ideas that many readers would consider important. No programmatic list can hope to be truly exhaustive. And any such list represents a hypothetical ideal of what a socialist government might do, were it to find itself in a position to do it. The question we must turn to now is what the political strategy might be that could actually bring such a situation about.

6

The Strategy

This book can't hope to offer a comprehensive road map to socialist victory. But before closing, we should consider some basic questions about who might be able to enact such a programme, how they would do it, and why they would do it. Before that, we must reflect on some of the historical obstacles that all actual socialist projects have faced.

Lessons from Failure

Conservative and liberal critics like to claim that socialism 'always fails', in contrast to the 'success' of capitalism. This is nonsense. For one thing, it's an idea based on the fallacy that socialism and capitalism are totally coherent and self-contained social systems. In fact, all modern societies have contained elements of capitalism and socialism, and it is only the elements of socialism that have made life tolerable for most human beings within those societies.

It is true that, so far, most attempts to replace capitalism with socialism as rapidly and extensively as possible, within particular countries, have been defeated. This is primarily because, from the beginning of the Russian Revolution to the recent experiences of Venezuela's socialist government, the United States and its allies have done everything in their power to ensure failure – from imposing economic embargoes to funding military coups against democratically elected governments. Venezuela's recent experiment in socialism has not failed because of some intrinsic problem with socialism: it has been severely compromised by the hostility of the United States and the collapse of the international oil price, upon which that country's economic independence has always relied.

But it is also true that attempts to transition to socialism too rapidly have often been made at the expense of real democracy, as centralised socialist regimes tried to impose revolutionary change on populations that were not ready for it. And in fact this is exactly what was predicted by Bakunin,[1] the anarchist leader who debated revolutionary strategy with Marx in the 1870s, and by the left-wing socialists who criticised Lenin and the Bolshevisks in revolutionary Russia.[2] They all argued, correctly, that socialism could be built only with the full participation and active support of the majority of a population, and that the centralised, top-down strategies advocated by Marx and Lenin would lead to authoritarian dictatorships.

The experience of the most successful attempts at building democratic socialist institutions – from the United States and the United Kingdom in the 1930s and 1940s to countries such as Sweden, Slovenia and Costa Rica in more recent decades – suggests a number of key observations. It suggests that avoiding or neutralising the hostile attention of capitalist powers is crucial to the success of socialist endeavours: most of these countries have managed to avoid the United States' taking a direct interest in their socialist and social–democratic projects – which, for various specific reasons, it did not. In the twenty-first century, this will mean that any social-ist project (at least outside the United States) must seek allies around the world and find ways to enable socialist movements and governments to cooperate productively with one another.

This history also suggests that socialism can be built only with the support of a real majority of a population, and that building this real support among diverse social groups is more important than building the numerical strength of any one party, organisation or union. It suggests that socialism cannot be built all at once, but that it must be built in full awareness of the mortal danger that capitalism always poses to democracy.

Revolutionaries following the vanguard strategies of Lenin have often tried to impose socialism from above, far too quickly, after a small revolutionary force had captured military and state power. They have generally assumed that the masses would eventually learn to thank them for it; but this has never happened. At the same time, mainstream social democrats have often convinced themselves that capitalism could be tamed and civilised rather than merely contained and gradually transformed. . As a result, many social–democratic reforms have been reversed or turned into new opportunities for capital accumulation, once capitalists had got used to them and figured out how to turn them to their advantage. Only a socialism that is fully democratic, strategically pragmatic, but decisively anti-capitalist in its orientation can avoid all these historical pitfalls.

Who Will Do It?

All prior history suggests that a programme such as the one envisaged here can be implemented only by a powerful social movement that is also capable of forming governments. A movement of this kind must be organised in communities, in workplaces, in educational institutions, and everywhere else where people meet and talk to one another. Today it must be organised online, exerting influence at every possible site, from local neighbourhood Facebook groups to online gaming platforms. It needs media outlets, it needs publishers, it needs community organisers and philosophers. It also needs to have significant influence within political parties.

Such a movement cannot be simply composed of members of one particular social group. It will have to contain most of the working class, precarious graduates, middle-class professionals (especially in the public sector) and that large slice of the 'new petite bourgeoisie' that now sees its children's prospects dwindling as they enter adulthood and even early middle age, unable to afford homes or to secure stable careers. Of course, bringing together such a diverse coalition will always be a challenge and will often require us to emphasise the things we have in common – our shared material interest in a fairer, cleaner, less capitalistic world – rather than the cultural and social factors that divide us.

By the same token, such a movement must draw heavily on the legacy of various movements – against racism and imperialism, of radical anti-racism, and for women's liberation and gay liberation.[3] This is important partly because capitalism is not the only problem or the only oppressive set of practices and relationships that we face in the twenty-first century. Women, people of colour, gay and lesbian people, trans people, people with disabilities and many others face specific difficulties that can't be entirely explained by the capitalist logic of accumulation, but that any meaningful socialist politics must address. At the same time, the oppressive social relations that disempower specific groups of people have negative consequences for everybody.

This is why it is a catastrophic mistake to assume that issues of gender, race and sexuality are merely 'identity' issues, of interest only to women, people of colour or sexual 'minorities'. The expectations placed on men, on straight people, and even on white people to conform to a narrow set of norms in order to play the roles ascribed to them can be oppressively limiting in their consequences (although clearly not as oppressive as they are for the groups most disempowered by them, nor oppressive in the same way).

119

But nobody actually stands to gain more from the programme set out in the previous chapter than do members of these specifically oppressed groups. For example: redistributing work – including domestic work – would not solve all of women's problems, but would solve more problems for women than for anyone else. Making the police and the schools genuinely accountable to their communities while giving them the capacity to serve these communities effectively would help everybody, but no one would benefit more than urban black and ethnic minority communities.[4]

Why Would They Do It? Radical Freedom

Bringing together such diverse groups and traditions will not be easy, and it would not be realistic to expect them to unite around some absolutely coherent ideology. But any such movement needs some sense of why it is coming together at all – what its big ideas are, what feelings and hopes its diverse constituents share. It is often said that the ideal all socialists share is the ideal of 'equality'. But I think an even more fundamental principle must animate the movement for twenty-first-century socialism: the shared goal of radical freedom.

The black freedom struggle, the women's liberation and the gay liberation movements were key driving forces in the cultural revolution of the 1960s and 1970s. Between them they proposed to create a society that would feel very different from the conformist, hierarchical culture of the post-war period. In particular, these movements were all motivated by a radical concept of liberation, very different from the classical liberal concept of freedom that still dominates western culture today.[5]

The liberal tradition treats freedom as something that only individuals can have: a capacity that they exercise alone. As such, it tends to assume that personal freedom is always limited by the individual's belonging to groups. Communities, families and the state are thought of as institutions that *stop* individuals from doing things, rather than helping them.[6]

But the radical tradition recognises that actually meaningful freedom is always the freedom to do something or to express something, and that doing or expressing things is always, in very different ways, a social activity. Belonging to groups doesn't limit our freedom: we don't have any meaningful freedom except as members of social groups. What matters is the way those groups are organised. This is a politics that is *libertarian*, because it believes in maximising freedom wherever possible; but it is not *liberal*, because it understands that people are more than just individuals to be set free from the bonds imposed on them by groups. From a libertarian socialist perspective, humans are social creatures who must be free to organise their relationships with others in as many creative ways as possible.[7] The goal of a libertarian and democratic twenty-first-century socialism is to organise our social lives in a such a way as to maximise our real freedom.

How Would They Do It? Parties and Movements

Political parties will obviously have a significant part to play in all this, at least for the foreseeable future. They have a crucial role in fighting elections and seeking governmental office. But this is only one aspect of their fundamental role, which is two-fold. On the one hand, parties serve to coordinate the activities and demands of different groups and political constituencies for as long as it takes to achieve some specific political objectives. On the other, they offer a sense of political identity and belonging to those different groups and constituencies, marking the difference between one political camp and another.[8]

In chapter 3 I outlined some of the problems with

the very idea of a representative democracy based on political parties in our complex postmodern world. But this does not mean that political parties can simply be dispensed with. Rather it means that the notion of a political party as no more than a vehicle that supports a group of professional politicians who 'represent' their supporters is no longer sustainable. Parties must be organisations that enable their members to act together, think together and make decisions together. If they are to do that effectively, however, then they must adapt to changing circumstances and use the best methods available to them.[9]

Political parties are necessary for fighting elections. But parties alone cannot effect lasting social change. Such change does not ultimately depend on the outcome of elections, but on the real balance of forces in society: the relative strength of different social groups, which ones among them have the most power, which ones among them are the best resourced and the best organised. In the early 1970s, for example, right-wing governments in the United Kingdom and United States toyed with the idea of implementing early forms of a neoliberal programme but didn't dare, because of the backlash they feared from voters, organised labour, and the youth.[10] Conversely, no left-wing government has ever implemented a successful reform programme without a large-scale movement of workers, citizens and activists that supported it, challenged its opponents in the media, and was willing to stand up to threats of economic blackmail from capitalists. At the end of the day, it's not who is in government that matters; it's the overall balance of forces in society.

Building a Movement

Building a movement is an organic process that cannot follow any prescribed blueprint. But there are some general features of successful movement building that we can observe from the history of the twentieth century, when movements such as Women's Liberation achieved astonish social changes (despite their limitations). Crucially, building a genuine movement is *never* simply a matter of campaigning for specific, localised issues and objectives. The difference between a campaign and a movement is that a movement will always involve some general questioning of the nature of contemporary society, rather than focusing on specific features of it that need to change. The difference between a labour movement and a trade union is that the movement challenges the very nature of class relations in a capitalist society. The difference between the women's movement and single-issue campaigns (over issues such as women's right to equal pay) is that the movement called into question the fundamental ways in which people are socialised into particular gender roles, along with the economic, political, cultural and psychological effects of that socialisation.

This kind of questioning means that political education is always a crucial feature of movement building. In the process of questioning society, movements will necessarily develop new concepts, new terminologies, new ways of thinking about the past, the present and the future. Generating such ideas and communicating them is an essential part of movement building. For example, the politicisation of the labour movement in the late nineteenth century depended in part on the circulation and popularisation of a Marxian critique of capitalism among the movement's most militant members. In the United Kingdom, one of the most obvious symptoms of the weakness of the political left since the 1980s has been the lack of energy devoted to such efforts of radical education and knowledge production.

Political education is crucial to movement building because it enable ideas generated by the movement to be passed along into the wider culture of a society. Again, the history of the women's liberation movement is a good example. Books, discussion circles and reading groups were as important to its spread as any other organisational vehicles, and its power was exercised by way of influencing writers, musicians, TV producers and educators as much as politicians and corporate executives. In 1965, even in 'modern', 'liberal' countries such as the United States and the United Kingdom, the idea that women's historical subordination should be ended was a fringe view, even on the political left. By 2005, even though there was a long way to go to achieve anything like real equality, its desirability as an objective had become widely accepted at nearly every level of society.

Any movement that wants to challenge the domination of capitalism and the legacy of neoliberalism must be equally ambitious and wide-ranging in its scope. It must seek to confront in every way the idea that humans are, or should be, inherently competitive, individualistic and asocial, while also refusing to have any truck with nationalist, racist or misogynistic thinking. It must take this perspective into workplaces and political parties, but also into the domains of education, music, television, cinema, literature and philosophy.[11]

Such work cannot be undertaken by just *one* organisation or type of organisation in any given context. Twentieth-century socialism had a strong tendency to look for one right answer, one unitary vision of socialism, one single party of the working class to deliver it. That's why revolutionary parties so often divided into tiny sects and factions; if there can be only one true socialism, then no disagreement within a socialist party or movement can be tolerated.

In the complex field of twenty-first-century society, there is no way that this kind of dogmatism will lead to anything but failure. Only a pluralistic ecology of organisations, groups, projects and tendencies is going to be able to confront capitalist power in the many different contexts where it must be fought. After the cultural revolution of the 1960s, after the crisis of democracy brought on by neoliberalism, as we enter the next stages of the cybernetic revolution, socialism in the twenty-first century must be multicoloured, libertarian, democratic and strategic.

The world we live in today is the outcome of different, competing forces encountering one another. It is the product of the bloody history of colonialism. It was born in the smoke and heat of the industrial revolution, transformed again by the technological advances of our own time, driven by the capitalist quest for profit. But it was also made by millions who fought for freedom, joined unions, rebelled against empire, and questioned every assumption; who did science for the benefit of humanity, who loved nature, and who cared for the children, the sick and the old. One of those legacies will shape the history of the twenty-first century. Which one is entirely up to us.

Notes

1 Couze Venn, *After Capital* (London: SAGE, 2018).

Notes to Chapter 1

1 Raymond Williams, *Keywords: A Vocabulary of Culture and Society*, rev. edn (Oxford: Oxford University Press, 1985).
2 Eric Hobsbawm, *The Age of Revolution : Europe, 1789–1848* (London: Abacus, 1988).
3 Zygmunt Bauman, *Globalization: The Human Consequences* (Cambridge: Polity, 1998).
4 A. J. Veal, 'The Leisure Society, I: Myths and Misconceptions, 1960–1979', *World Leisure Journal* 53.3 (2011): 206–27, doi: 10.1080/04419057.2011.606826; Joshua Krook, 'Whatever Happened to the 15-Hour Workweek?', The Conversation, http://theconversation.com/whatever-happened-to-the-15-hour-workweek-84781.

5 Karl Marx and C. J. Arthur, *Marx's* Capital: *A Student Edition* (London: Lawrence & Wishart, 1993).
6 Ibid.
7 Andre Vladimirovich Anikin, *A Science in Its Youth: Pre-Marxian Political Economy* (Moscow: Progress Publishers, 1979).
8 Andrea Fumagalli et al., 'Digital Labour in the Platform Economy: The Case of Facebook', *Sustainability* 10.6 (2018), article 1757, doi: 10.3390/su10061757.
9 Eric Hobsbawm, *The Age of Capital, 1848–1875* (London: Abacus, 1988).
10 Marx and Arthur, *Marx's* Capital.
11 Eric J. Hobsbawm, *The Age of Empire, 1875–1914* (New York: Pantheon Books, 1987).
12 Raymond Williams, 'Advertising: The Magic System', *Advertising & Society Review* 1.1 (2000): 320–36, doi: 10.1353/asr.2000.0016.
13 Melissa Benn, *School Wars: The Battle for Britain's Education* (London: Verso, 2012).
14 jemgilbert, '"Neoliberalism" and "Capitalism": What's the Difference?', Jeremygilbertwriting (blog), 14 July 2015, https://jeremygilbertwriting.word press.com/2015/07/14/neoliberalism-and-capitalism-whats-the-difference; Jeremy Gilbert, 'What Kind of Thing Is "Neoliberalism"?', *New Formations* 80–81 (2013): 7–12, doi: 10.3898/nEWF.80/81. IntroductIon.2013.
15 Mark Olsen, John Codd and Anne-Marie O'Neill, *Education Policy: Globalization, Citizenship and*

Democracy (London: SAGE, 2004); Benn, *School Wars*.

16 Colin Crouch, *Post-Democracy* (Cambridge: Polity, 2004).

17 Barry Hindess and Paul Q. Hirst, *Mode of Production and Social Formation: An Auto-Critique of Pre-Capitalist Modes of Production* (London: Palgrave Macmillan, 1977).

18 Natalie Fenton, *Digital, Political, Radical* (Cambridge: Polity, 2018); James Curran, Julian Petley, and Ivor Gaber, *Culture Wars: The Media and the British Left* (Edinburgh: Edinburgh University Press, 2005).

19 Jo Littler, *Against Meritocracy (Open Access): Culture, Power and Myths of Mobility* (London: Routledge, 2017).

20 The idea that capitalism has a basically parasitic relationship with the 'real economy' of people engaged in general social, creative and communicative activities finds one of is most elaborated theoretical expressions in the recent work of Hardt and Negri; but good empirical analyses can also be found in the work of radical economists, anthropologists, geogrphers and political scientists who study practices of 'commoning'. See, for example, Michael Hardt and Antonio Negri, *Empire* (Cambridge, MA: Harvard University Press, 2001); Michael Hardt and Antonio Negri, *Commonwealth* (Cambridnge, MA: Harvard University Press, 2009); David Bollier and Silke Helfrich, *The Wealth of the Commons: A World Beyond Market and State* (Amherst: Levellers Press, 2014).

21 Leigh Phillips and Michal Rozworski, *The People's Republic of Walmart: How the World's Biggest Corporations Are Laying the Foundation for Socialism* (London: Verso, 2019).

22 Mariana Mazzucato, *The Entrepreneurial State: Debunking Public vs. Private Sector Myths* (London: Penguin, 2018).

23 Douglas Rushkoff, *Team Human* (New York: W. W. Norton, 2019).

24 This is an imaginary passage. See also Crawford Brough Macpherson, *The Political Theory of Possessive Individualism : Hobbes to Locke* (Oxford: Oxford University Press, 1988).

25 Domenico Losurdo, *Liberalism: A Counter-History* (London: Verso Books, 2014).

26 Ibid.

27 Michel Foucault, Arnold I. Davidson and Graham Burchell, *The Birth of Biopolitics: Lectures at the Collège de France, 1978–1979* (Mannheim: Springer, 2008); William Davis, *The Limits of Neoliberalism* (London: SAGE, 2014).

28 Stuart Hall and Alan O'Shea, 'Common-Sense Neoliberalism', *Soundings* 55.55 (2013): 9–25, doi: 10.3898/136266213809450194; Jeremy Gilbert, *Neoliberal Culture* (London: Lawrence & Wishart, 2016); Jim McGuigan, *Neoliberal Culture* (London: Springer, 2016); Patricia Ventura, *Neoliberal Culture: Living with American Neoliberalism* (New York: Routledge, 2016).

29 Jeremy Gilbert, *Common Ground: Democracy and*

Collectivity in an Age of Individualism (London: Pluto Press, 2014).

30 David Harvey, *A Brief History of Neoliberalism* (Oxford: Oxford University Press, 2007).

Notes to Chapter 2

1 Leigh Phillips and Michal Rozworski, The People's Republic of Walmart: How the World's Biggest Corporations Are Laying the Foundation for Socialism (London: Verso, 2019).

2 Jeremy Gilbert, *Common Ground: Democracy and Collectivity in an Age of Individualism* (London: Pluto Press, 2014).

3 John Curl, *For All the People: Uncovering the Hidden History of Cooperation, Cooperative Movements, and Communalism in America* (Oakland, CA: PM Press, 2009).

4 James Robertson, 'The Life and Death of Yugoslav Socialism', *Jacobin*, 17 July 2017, https://jacobin mag.com/2017/07/yugoslav-socialism-tito-self-man agement-serbia-balkans.

5 'Feasible Socialism', Socialist Health Association, 25 August 1994, https://www.sochealth.co.uk/social ism/feasible-socialism.

6 'The NHS Is the British Institution That Brits Are Second-Most Proud of – After the Fire Brigade', YouGov, https://yougov.co.uk/topics/politics/articles -reports/2018/07/04/nhs-british-institution-brits-are- second-most-prou.

7 Paul Addison, *The Road to 1945: British Politics and*

the Second World War, rev. edn (London: Random House, 2011).

8 'We Are Going to "Tredegarise" You', Almost History, http://www.vaguelyinteresting.co.uk/we-are-going-to-tredegarise-you.

9 Julian Tudor Hart, book review of Marvin Rintala, *Creating the National Health Service: Aneurin Bevan and the Medical Lords* (London: Frank Cass, 2003), *International Journal of Epidemiology* 32.6 (2003): 1121–22, doi: 10.1093/ije/dyg331.

10 Hywel Francis and David Smith, *The Fed: History of the South Wales Miners in the Twentieth Century* (London: Lawrence & Wishart, 1980).

11 Mike Gerrard, *A Stifled Voice* (London: Pen Press, 2006).

12 Lee Marshall, '"Let's Keep Music Special. F—Spotify": On-Demand Streaming and the Controversy over Artist Royalties', *Creative Industries Journal* 8.2 (2015): 177–89, doi: 10.1080/17510694.2015.1096618.

13 David Bollier, 'A New Politics of the Commons', *Renewal*, http://www.renewal.org.uk/articles/a-new-politics-of-the-commons; David Bollier and Silke Helfrich, *The Wealth of the Commons: A World Beyond Market and State* (Amherst: Levellers Press, 2014); Michel Bauwens, Vasilis Kostakis, and Alex Pazaitis, *Peer to Peer: The Commons Manifesto* (London: University of Westminster Press, 2019); Guido Ruivenkamp and Andy Hilton, *Perspectives on Commoning: Autonomist Principles and Practices* (London: Zed Books, 2017); Jeremy Gilbert,

Common Ground: Democracy and Collectivity in an Age of Individualism (London: Pluto Press, 2014).

14 Gilbert, *Common Ground*.

Notes to Chapter 3

1 Paul Mason, *Postcapitalism: A Guide to Our Future* (London: Penguin, 2015).

2 Fred Turner, *From Counterculture to Cyberculture: Stewart Brand, the Whole Earth Network, and the Rise of Digital Utopianism* (Chicago, IL: University of Chicago Press, 2010); Fred Turner, *The Democratic Surround: Multimedia and American Liberalism from World War II to the Psychedelic Sixties* (Chicago, IL: University of Chicago Press, 2013); Steven Levy, *Hackers: Heroes of the Computer Revolution*, 25th anniversary edn (New York: O'Reilly Media, 2010).

3 Thomas Rid, *Rise of the Machines: The Lost History of Cybernetics* (London: Scribe Publications, 2016).

4 Edward Palmer Thompson, *The Making of the English Working Class* (London: Victor Gollancz, 1965); Howard Zinn, *A People's History of the United States* (New York: Harper Perennial, 2015); Eric J. Hobsbawm, *The Age of Empire, 1875–1914* (New York: Pantheon Books, 1987); Eric J. Hobsbawm, *The Age of Extremes: The Short Twentieth Century, 1914–1991* (London: Michael Joseph, 1994); Selina Todd, *The People: The Rise and Fall of the Working Class, 1910–2010* (London: John Murray, 2014).

5 Donald Sassoon, *One Hundred Years of Socialism: The Western European Left in the Twentieth Century* (New York: New York Press, 1996).

6 Jane McAlevey, *No Shortcuts: Organizing for Power in the New Gilded Age* (Oxford: Oxford University Press, 2016).

7 Sassoon, *One Hundred Years of Socialism*.

8 Vijay Prashad, *The Poorer Nations: A Possible History of the Global South* (London: Verso Books, 2014); Quinn Slobodian, *Globalists: The End of Empire and the Birth of Neoliberalism* (Cambridge, MA: Harvard University Press, 2018).

9 Prashad, *The Poorer Nations*; Slobodian, *Globalists*.

10 Stuart Hall and Martin Jacques, *New Times: The Changing Face of Politics in the 1990s* (London: Verso, 1989); Manuel Castells, *The Rise of the Network Society* (Oxford: Wiley Blackwell, 2011); Zygmunt Bauman, *Liquid Modernity* (Cambridge: Polity, 2013); Zygmunt Bauman, *Community: Seeking Safety in an Insecure World* (Cambridge: Polity, 2013); Richard Sennett, *The Corrosion of Character: The Personal Consequences of Work in the New Capitalism* (London: W. W. Norton, 2011); Richard Sennett, *The Culture of the New Capitalism* (London: Yale University Press, 2007).

11 Arthur Marwick, *The Sixties: Cultural Revolution in Britain, France, Italy, and the United States, c. 1958–c. 1974* (London: A&C Black, 2011).

12 Sheila Rowbotham, *Promise of a Dream: Remembering the Sixties* (London: Verso, 2001);

Todd Gitlin, *The Sixties: Years of Hope, Days of Rage* (New York: Random House Publishing Group, 2013).

13 Sam Binkley, *Getting Loose: Lifestyle Consumption in the 1970s* (Durham, NC: Duke University Press, 2007).

14 Yohuru Williams, *Rethinking the Black Freedom Movement* (London: Routledge, 2015); Charles V. Hamilton and Kwame Ture, *Black Power: Politics of Liberation in America* (New York: Knopf Doubleday Publishing Group, 2011).

15 Sheila Rowbotham, *The Past Is before Us: Feminism in Action Since the 1960s* (London: Pandora, 1989); Alice Echols, *Daring to Be Bad: Radical Feminism in America, 1967–1975* (Minneapolis: University of Minnesota Press, 1989).

16 Zygmunt Bauman, *Postmodernity and Its Discontents* (Cambridge: Polity, 2013).

17 Adam Becker, *What Is Real? The Unfinished Quest for the Meaning of Quantum Physics* (London: Hachette, 2018).

18 Jean-François Lyotard, *The Postmodern Condition: A Report on Knowledge* (Minneapolis: University of Minnesota Press, 1984).

19 Jeremy Gilbert, 'Postmodernity and the Crisis of Democracy', Open Democracy, 2009, https://www.opendemocracy.net/en/postmodernity-and-the-crisis-of-democracy.

20 Jeremy Gilbert, *Common Ground: Democracy and Collectivity in an Age of Individualism* (London: Pluto Press, 2014).

21 Carole Pateman, *Participation and Democratic Theory* (Cambridge: Cambridge University Press, 1975); Donald Reid, *Opening the Gates: The Lip Affair, 1968–1981* (London: Verso, 2018); Francesca Polletta, *Freedom Is an Endless Meeting: Democracy in American Social Movements* (Chicago, IL: University of Chicago Press, 2004).

22 Stuart Hall et al., *Policing the Crisis: Mugging, the State and Law and Order* (London: Macmillan International Higher Education, 2013).

23 Andrew Gamble, *The Free Economy and the Strong State: The Politics of Thatcherism* (Durham, NC: Duke University Press, 1988).

24 Tariq Ali, *Pirates of the Caribbean: Axis of Hope* (London: Verso, 2008).

25 Colin Crouch, *The Strange Non-Death of Neo-Liberalism* (Cambridge: Polity, 2013).

26 Alison Hearn, 'Meat, Mask, Burden', *Journal of Consumer Culture* 8.2 (2008): 197–217, doi: 10.1177/1469540508090086; Stuart Hall and Alan O'Shea, 'Common-Sense Neoliberalism', *Soundings* 55.55 (2013): 9–25, https://doi.org/10.3898/136266213809450194.

27 John Clarke and Janet Newman, *The Managerial State: Power, Politics and Ideology in the Remaking of Social Welfare* (London: SAGE, 1997); Timothy Bewes and Jeremy Gilbert, *Cultural Capitalism: Politics after New Labour* (London: Lawrence & Wishart, 2000); Mark Fisher and Jeremy Gilbert, 'Reclaim Modernity: Beyond Markets beyond Machines', Compass, 2014, http://www.compas

sonline.org.uk/publications/reclaiming-modernity-beyond-markets-beyond-machines.

28 Ron Formisano, *American Oligarchy: The Permanent Political Class* (Champaign: University of Illinois Press, 2017).

29 Neal Lawson, *All Consuming* (London: Penguin, 2009).

30 David Graeber, *Bullshit Jobs: A Theory* (London: Simon & Schuster, 2018).

31 Robert D. Putnam, *Bowling Alone: The Collapse and Revival of American Community* (London: Simon & Schuster, 2001).

32 Lynne Segal, *Radical Happiness: Moments of Collective Joy* (London: Verso, 2018); Douglas Rushkoff, *Team Human* (New York: W. W. Norton, 2019); Gilbert, *Common Ground*.

Notes to Chapter 4

1 Naomi Klein, *This Changes Everything: Capitalism vs The Climate* (London: Simon & Schuster, 2014).

2 Leigh Phillips, *Austerity Ecology and the Collapse-Porn Addicts: A Defence Of Growth, Progress, Industry and Stuff* (London: Zero Books, 2015).

3 Jonathan Watts (Global environment editor), 'We Have 12 Years to Limit Climate Change Catastrophe, Warns UN', *Guardian*, 8 October 2018, https://www.theguardian.com/environment/2018/oct/08/global-warming-must-not-exceed-15c-warns-landmark-un-report.

4 Riley E. Dunlap and Aaron M. McCright, *Organized Climate Change Denial* (Oxford: Oxford University Press, 2011), doi: 10.1093/oxfor dhb/9780199566600.003.0010.

5 Karl Marx and Friedrich Engels, *The Communist Manifesto* (London: Penguin Adult, 2002).

6 'Employment and Employee Types', Office for National Statistics, 2019, https://www.ons.gov.uk/employmen-tandlabourmarket/peopleinwork/employmentand employeetypes.

7 Mike Savage, *Social Class in the 21st Century* (London: Penguin, 2015).

8 The account of changes to the class structure that I'm offering here is partly based on sources such as Savage (2015), but is modified by my assumption that certain differences and commonalities not normally taken into account by such sources are of great political importance – most notably the differential dependence of various social groups on the public sector, for either employment or essential services. Although my account is simpler and more schematic than that of Savage and others, I think it is congruent with theirs.

9 Savage, *Social Class in the 21st Century*.

10 David Graeber, *The Utopia of Rules: On Technology, Stupidity, and the Secret Joys of Bureaucracy* (New York: Melville House, 2015).

11 Nick Srnicek and Alex Williams, *Inventing the Future: Postcapitalism and a World Without Work* (London: Verso, 2015).

12 'Average Actual Weekly Hours of Work for Full-Time Workers (Seasonally Adjusted)', Office for

National Statistics, 2019, https://www.ons.gov.uk/
employmentandlabourmarket/peopleinwork/earn
ingsandworkinghours/timeseries/ybuy/lms.

13 Of course, astute commentators could already see where things were going: Tiziana Terranova, *Network Culture: Politics for the Information Age* (London: Pluto Press, 2004).

14 Nick Srnicek, *Platform Capitalism* (Cambridge: Polity, 2017).

15 Shoshana Zuboff, *The Age of Surveillance Capitalism: The Fight for a Human Future at the New Frontier of Power* (London: Profile Books, 2019).

16 'The Cambridge Analytica Files', *Guardian*, 17 March 2019, https://www.theguardian.com/news/ series/cambridge-analytica-files/all.

17 Ben Sellers, '#JezWeDid: From Red Labour to Jeremy Corbyn: A Tale from Social Media', #JezWeCan: The World Turned Upside Down, 27 September 2015, https://theworldturnedupsidedownne.word press.com/2015/09/27/jezwedid-from-red-labour-to- jeremy-corbyn-a-tale-from-social-media.

18 Joss Hands, @ *Is for Activism: Dissent, Resistance and Rebellion in a Digital Culture* (London: Pluto Press, 2011); Paolo Gerbaudo, *Tweets and the Streets: Social Media and Contemporary Activism* (London: Pluto Press, 2012); Paolo Gerbaudo, *The Digital Party: Political Organisation and Online Democracy* (London: Pluto Press, 2018).

19 Angela Nagle, *Kill All Normies: Online Culture Wars from 4chan and tumblr to Trump and the Alt- Right* (London: Zero Books, 2017).

20 Zuboff, *The Age of Surveillance Capitalism*.
21 Mark Blyth, *Austerity: The History of a Dangerous Idea* (Oxford: Oxford University Press, 2015).
22 John Lanchester (no title), *Guardian*, 21 October 2008, https://www.theguardian.com/business/2008/oct/20/creditcrunch-marketturmoil-globaleconomy.
23 Blyth, *Austerity*.
24 Geoff Tilley, '17-Year Wage Squeeze the Worst in Two Hundred Years', TUC, 2018, https://www.tuc.org.uk/blogs/17-year-wage-squeeze-worst-two-hundred-years.
25 Keir Milburn, *Generation Left* (Cambridge: Polity, 2019).
26 Laurie Ouellette and James Hay, *Better Living through Reality TV: Television and Post-Welfare Citizenship* (Malden, MA: Blackwell, 2008).
27 Costas Lapavitsas, *Profiting without Producing: How Finance Exploits Us All* (London: Verso, 2013).
28 Milburn, *Generation Left*.

Notes to Chapter 5

1 Neal Lawson, 'Dare More Democracy', Compass, 2003, https://www.compassonline.org.uk/publications/dare-more-democracy.
2 Jeremy Gilbert, *Common Ground: Democracy and Collectivity in an Age of Individualism* (London: Pluto Press, 2014).
3 Paul Mason, *Postcapitalism: A Guide to Our Future* (London: Penguin, 2015).
4 Andrew Robinson, 'In Theory Bakunin vs Marx',

Ceasefire Magazine, 1 July 2011, https://cease-firemagazine.co.uk/in-theory-bakunin-2; Mikhail Bakunin, *Marxism, Freedom and the State* (London: Freedom Press, 1950), in digital version at https://www.marxists.org/reference/archive/bakunin/works/mf-state/index.htm.

5 G. D. H. Cole, *Guild Socialism Restated* (London: Routledge, 2017); Paul Q. Hirst, *Associative Democracy: New Forms of Economic and Social Governance* (Cambridge: Polity, 1994).

6 James Robertson, 'The Life and Death of Yugoslav Socialism', *Jacobin*, 17 July 2017, https://jacobin mag.com/2017/07/yugoslav-socialism-tito-self-man agement-serbia-balkans.

7 Eden Medina, *Cybernetic Revolutionaries: Technology and Politics in Allende's Chile* (Cambridge, MA: MIT Press, 2011); Eden Medina, 'The Cybersyn Revolution', *Jacobin*, 27 April 2015, https://jacobin-mag.com/2015/04/allende-chile-beer-medina-cyber-syn.

8 David Harvey, *A Brief History of Neoliberalism* (Oxford: Oxford University Press, 2007).

9 'Europe's Co-Op Boom', *Red Pepper*, 16 June 2010, https://www.redpepper.org.uk/europe-s-co-op-boom.

10 David Harvey, 'The Right to the City', *New Left Review* 53 (2008): 23–40, https://newleftreview.org/issues/II53/articles/david-harvey-the-right-to-the-city.

11 'The Green New Deal', New Economics Foundation, https://neweconomics.org/campaigns/green-new-deal; Jane McAlevey, 'Organizing to Win a Green

New Deal', Jacobin, 2019, https://jacobinmag. com/2019/03/green-new-deal-union-organizing-jobs.

12 Damian Carrington, 'Tree Planting "Has Mind-Blowing Potential" to Tackle Climate Crisis', *Guardian*, 4 July 2019, https://www.theguardian. com / environment / 2019 / jul / 04 / planting - billions - trees - best - tackle - climate - crisis - scientists - canopy - emissions.

13 'Mayday 23: World Population Becomes More Urban Than Rural', ScienceDaily, 25 May 2007, https://www. sciencedaily.com/releases/2007/05/070525000642. htm.

14 Harvey, 'The Right to the City'.

15 'Socialize Finance', https://jacobinmag.com/2016/11/ finance - banks - capitalism - markets - socialism - plan ning. See also James Meadway, 'Corbynomics: Where Next?', posted on the author's blog at Medium Corporation on 9 September 2015, https://medium. com / @james . meadway / corbynomics - where - next - 15139af74c52.

16 Mark Fisher and Jeremy Gilbert, 'Reclaim Modernity: Beyond Markets beyond Machines', Compass, 2014, http : / / www . compassonline . org . uk / publications / reclaiming - modernity - beyond - markets - beyond - machines.

17 Hilary Wainwright, *Reclaim the State: Experiments in Popular Democracy* (London: Verso, 2003); Hilary Wainwright, *A New Politics from the Left* (Cambridge: Polity, 2018); Neal, 'Dare More Democracy'.

18 Michael Fielding and Peter Moss, *Radical Education*

and the Common School: A Democratic Alternative (London: Routledge, 2010).

19 Melissa Benn and Janet Downs, *The Truth about Our Schools: Exposing the Myths, Exploring the Evidence* (London: Routledge, 2015); Melissa Benn, *Life Lessons* (London: Verso Books, 2018).

20 Nuala Burgess, 'Ban School League Tables: They're Not Just Misleading, They're Harmful', *Guardian*, 26 January 2019, https://www.theguardian.com/commentisfree/2019/jan/26/school-league-tables-research-grammar.

21 UCL, 'IGP's Social Prosperity Network Publishes the UK's First Report on Universal Basic Services', UCL Institute for Global Prosperity, 11 October 2017, https://www.ucl.ac.uk/bartlett/igp/news/2017/oct/igps-social-prosperity-network-publishes-uks-first-report-universal-basic-services.

22 Erik Olin Wright, *Envisioning Real Utopias* (London: Verso, 2010).

23 Thomas M. Hanna, Joe Guinan, and Joe Bilsborough, 'The "Preston Model" and the Modern Politics of Municipal Socialism', Open Democracy, 2017, https://www.opendemocracy.net/en/opendemocracyuk/preston-model-and-modern-politics-of-municipal-socialism.

24 Nick Srnicek, *Platform Capitalism* (Cambridge: Polity, 2017).

25 Vasilis Kostakis and Michel Bauwens, 'Cooperativism in the Digital Era, or How to Form a Global Counter-Economy | Open Democracy, 2017, https://www.opendemocracy.net/en/digitaliberties/coopera

tivism-in-digital-era-or-how-to-form-global-counter-economy.

26 Gilbert, *Common Ground*.

27 Wainwright, *Reclaim the State*; Fisher and Gilbert, 'Reclaim Modernity'.

28 Christine Berry and Joe Guinan, *People Get Ready: Preparing for a Corbyn Government* (London: OR Books, 2019).

29 Jane McAlevey, *No Shortcuts: Organizing for Power in the New Gilded Age* (Oxford: Oxford University Press, 2016); Paul Mason, *Live Working or Die Fighting: How the Working Class Went Global* (Chicago, IL: Haymarket Books, 2010).

30 '1. Is Work in Crisis? Helen Hester' (blog), Autonomy website, 2019, http://autonomy.work/portfolio/helen-hester-response.

31 Nick Srnicek and Alex Williams, *Inventing the Future: Postcapitalism and a World Without Work* (London: Verso, 2015)

32 Stuart Lansley and Howard Reed, *Basic Income for All: From Desirability to Feasibility* (London: Compass, 2019), http://www.compassonline.org.uk/wp-content/uploads/2019/03/Compass_BasicIncomeForAll_2019.pdf.

33 Raymond Williams, *Communications* (London: Chatto & Windus, 1966); Fisher and Gilbert, 'Reclaim Modernity'; Media Reform Coalition, 'Media Manifesto 2019' (blog), MRC website, 21 March 2019, https://www.mediareform.org.uk/blog/media-manifesto-2019.

34 James Curran and Jean Seaton, *Power without*

Responsibility: Press, Broadcasting and the Internet in Britain (London: Routledge, 2002).

35 Dan Hind, *The Return of the Public: Democracy, Power and the Case for Media Reform* (London: Verso, 2012).

Notes to Chapter 6

1 Michail Aleksandrovi Bakunin, *Marxism, Freedom and the State* (London: Freedom Press, 1950); 'In Theory Bakunin vs Marx'.

2 John Medhurst, *No Less Than Mystic* (London: Repeater, 2017).

3 Sheila Rowbotham, Lynne Segal, and Hilary Wainwright, *Beyond the Fragments: Feminism and the Making of Socialism* (London: Merlin Press, 2013).

4 Charles V. Hamilton and Kwame Ture, *Black Power: Politics of Liberation in America* (New York: Knopf Doubleday Publishing Group, 2011); Keeanga-Yamahtta Taylor, *From #BlackLivesMatter to Black Liberation* (Chicago, IL: Haymarket Books, 2016).

5 Sheila Rowbotham, *Woman's Consciousness, Man's World* (London: Penguin, 1973); Hamilton and Ture, *Black Power*; Aubrey Walter, *Come Together: The Years of Gay Liberation, 1970–73* (London: Gay Men's Press, 1980).

6 Jeremy Gilbert, *Common Ground: Democracy and Collectivity in an Age of Individualism* (London: Pluto Press, 2014).

147

7 Jeremy Gilbert, 'Liberalism Does Not Imply Democracy', Open Democracy, 2009, https://www.opendemocracy.net/en/liberalism-does-not-imply-democracy.

8 Jodi Dean, *Crowds and Party* (London: Verso, 2016); Jeremy Gilbert, *Anticapitalism and Culture: Radical Theory and Popular Politics* (Oxford: Berg, 2008).

9 Ken Spours, 'The Very Modern Prince: The 21st Century Political Party and the Political Formation', Compass, 2016, https://www.compassonline.org.uk/publications/the-very-modern-prince-the-21st-century-political-party-and-the-political-formation.

10 Stuart Hall et al., *Policing the Crisis: Mugging, the State and Law and Order* (London: Macmillan International Higher Education, 2013).

11 Gilbert, *Common Ground*.